40 Years of Letters to the Editor

Thanks Makeshia for your help and I hope you and yours have a great Christmas

Cletus Harvey

40 Years of Letters to the Editor

Cletus Harvey

Copyright © 2015 by Cletus Harvey

All rights reserved.

Printed in the United States of America

First Printing, 2015

ISBN 978-1-517-10562-4

Some names and details have been changed to protect the privacy of individuals.

Book design by Brad Harvey & Belinda Harvey

Cover design by Lacey Robinson

DEDICATION

This book is dedicated to Doris Ruth Harvey, my wonderful wife of 41 years. Of all the blessings I have had in my life, she has been the greatest.

CONTENTS

	Dedication	i
	Preface	ii
1	Tale Of Two Towns	1
2	Trip Back To A Dying Little West Texas Town	5
3	A Real Cowboy If Ever I Met One	9
4	Death Of A Cowboy	13
5	Young People Are Great	15
6	The Courage To Stay Put	17
7	A Dumb Commercial	19
8	Where The Real America Lies	21
9	A Matter Of Perspective	23
10	Card Of Thanks – Before	25
11	Card Of Thanks – After	26
12	Remembering Noble Shaw	27
13	A Story Idea	30
14	In Defense Of Farmers	32
15	A Little Girl Grows Up	34
16	Buck Jones, A True Hero	37
17	The Television Guide	39
18	Remembering Dr. Cravens	40
19	Clifford Martin Would Never Bow Down	41

20	P & Z In Good Hands	44
21	A Class Act Downtown	46
22	Impressed With JP Court	47
23	A World War II Museum	48
24	Sound Off (1)	50
25	Sound Off (2)	51
26	Nurses Are Heroes	52
27	His Mother's Story	55
28	A Leader Of Men Is Gone	59
29	Worsham's Retirement	61
30	Showtime	62
31	World's Greatest Guardian	63
32	A Letter To Her Daddy	65
33	A Requiem For Buckshot	66
34	A Honey Of A Car	68
35	The Sheriff's A Good Man	71
36	The Tale Of "Old Tuffy"	73
37	A Poem	75
38	Lola Berry, A True Lady	76
39	Why Didn't I Be More Neighborly Before It Was Too Late?	78
40	Take Care Of Mr. Smooth	81
41	End Of The Trail?	84

42	The Good Samaritan	87
43	Lessons From A Horse	91
44	Alarm System A Nice Sleep Aid	93
45	Youth Is A State Of Mind	94
46	Defending His Friends	96
47	We Goof Again	97
48	On The Traffic Lights	99
49	Obnoxious Stickers	101
50	Nothing To Debate On Torture	103
51	Mourning A Closing	105
52	Fixing The Soggy Newspaper	107
53	Thank You To Cletus Harvey	109
54	A Tribute To The Mayor	111
55	Unsung Heroes	113
56	In Loving Remembrance Of Rom Holmes	117
57	Words To Live By	119
58	A Possible Solution To The Problems With The U.S. Postal Service	121
59	Dream Comes True	122
60	Master Storyteller Spins Tales From The Graves In The Oldest Town In Texas	123
61	Recalling Anne Millard	125
62	Cracking Up In Houston	127
63	On The Barefoot Girl	130

64	Boomtown Memories	131
65	A Great Accomplishment	133
66	Chivalry Is Alive And Well	134
67	Neighbor's Peace And Quiet Is Broken	135
68	Defending Home Health Care	138
69	A Letter To Her Grandparents	141
70	Master Sgt. Billy Byrd	143
71	Excerpt From Article By Emily Taravella	145
72	A Rodeo Star?	147
73	Stimulus That Works	149
74	Efficient Court System	151
75	Writer A Fan Of Cletus Harvey's Letters To Editor	152
76	The Definition Of Integrity	153
77	Bring In The Rangers	155
78	Downtown Memories	157
79	Taking Up For "Real Nacogdoches Treasures"	159
80	Memory Loss From Rodeo Fall	161
81	Hates A Soggy Newspaper	163
82	Sgt. Harvey And His Little Chatterbox	164
83	Helping The Less Fortunate	167
	About The Author	iii

PREFACE

Forty-two years in the wonderful town of Nacogdoches has been very rewarding. There are some of the most interesting and real people here. They do not give up trying to make their town better. Our newspaper needs to complement the good ones and let our outstanding police force handle the bad.

1. TALE OF TWO TOWNS

There's nothing like a good story. Some folks call it a legend. I think you can add color to most any legend that you want, to kind of dress it up a little and make it more interesting to your readers. My stories usually contain a little action and a lot of color, but my information is quite accurate.

This legend, or tale, has been passed down for generations. Although we have no concrete evidence, the heritage of the oldest towns in Texas is based on the story of how Nacogdoches began. I've personally decided I believe this one.

Long, long ago, around 1400, just a few years before the Mexicans came, the Indians living in East Texas were members of the Caddo family and Hasinai Confederacy. The Hasinai word for friend was "tejas", which would later become "Texas". Now, one of the Caddoan Tribe lived right about where Milam is located today, near the Sabine River. The chief of that Caddoan Tribe had two sons. Some stories say that they were twins, but from my research I have determined that they were brothers who were about one year apart in age. One brother had very dark hair and extremely dark, sunburned skin. The other son had light hair and light skin. If they were twins they would probably have had the same skin type. Anyway, although I probably can't spell it, one of the sons was named Natchitoches, and the other was named Nacogdoches.

The time came when these two sons were required to set out to establish new tribes which they would lead. Both Natchitoches and Nacogdoches were given three days in which to locate their new settlement. Natchitoches, the older dark-complected brother, headed eastward for three days into the rising sun, while Nacogdoches, the younger and light-complected brother (and probably the best looking brother), set out westward for three days into the setting sun. Both brothers left with the people that were going to begin their new tribes.

Because the terrain was different, the brother headed toward the east settled approximately 6 to 8 miles closer to Milam. This settlement, located in Louisiana, is known as Natchitoches. The other brother made his settlement in what is now known as Nacogdoches. The two brothers set up a trading route that later became known as the El Camino Real. Many of our heroes, like Davy Crockett, Sam Houston and William Travis, came to Texas through that trading route.

They say that folks in Nacogdoches and Lufkin are the descendants of the fair skinned brother, and that those folks in Natchitoches are the descendants of the dark skinned fellow. They planted and harvested crops, made preserves from fruit, preserved meat, and tanned hides. Both tribes remained friendly and peaceful and buried their dead in mounds. That's where Mound Street in Nacogdoches gets its name.

Today the two towns are still similar, although we've destroyed just about all of the history – our brothers must have been dumb – but that's another story. So, that's the legend of the Caddoan brothers and the twin towns of Nacogdoches, Texas and Natchitoches, Louisiana, and how they got started.

Electra, Texas

2. TRIP BACK TO A DYING LITTLE WEST TEXAS TOWN

The near Panhandle town of Electra, Texas is almost gone now. It sprang to life in the early 1920's when W. T. Waggoner, while having some men try to find water for his cattle, hit a gushing oil well. He could not hold back the flow of starving farmers, adventurers, and high rollers that came. So he gave the surrounding mesquite land for them to form a town. It was called Electra after W. T.'s daughter. (She may have never seen the town; she preferred the high society world in Fort Worth.) The town never welcomed any other industry, and when oil went bust and the highway went around it, the town died.

It hurts to go back to my hometown now, but because the two wonderful people who brought me into this world are still there, I do return some. The following are some of my observations during a recent trip.

Little is left of the downtown. Remaining buildings (including The Last Picture Show) are just shells now. Many have been torn out, leaving empty spaces.

Sitting on the edge of this is the Dairy Queen. This is where the remaining people gather for warmth and companionship twice a day – those who have weathered the storms, and survived.

As I walk in with my father for the early morning coffee gathering, I already know how the conversation will run. One of the men at the big table of coffee drinkers will say "Hey Red (my father's still called Red although his hair has been white for years) – I see that kid is back again so that you will have to feed him." You are not invited to be seated, but you know that if you will find a chair and pull it over, someone will scoot over a little.

After a long silence and some serious coffee drinking, someone might say "It took me a year to make my money back after you bunch of sissies lost that game to Vernon that time." How can I defend myself? That was years ago.

But then after leaving the old folk and getting some amount of feeling of worth and confidence back, I go alone to the Hard Times Café.

The gathering here is of has-been drillers, roughnecks, tool pushers, pumpers, rig builders, pipeliners, and cowboys from the big ranches.

The old oil field people may still wear their hard hats, leave home before daybreak, and even pack a sack lunch as if they have a purpose that will last all day. The cowboys will be wearing their spurs and chaps and will have a trailer outside filled with an old saddle horse, both just waiting for him to go nowhere.

This is the way it always goes in there. I could stay gone for years and get this same reception.

If I entered and stood respectfully long enough someone would say "How you doing Harvey?" Now this did not mean that I can feel free to tell them all how I am really doing. It merely means that if I want to find a chair and will not try to join in any conversation that they might be having, I will be tolerated. Since I knew that I wouldn't be talking, I seated myself so that I could see as much as possible.

As it turned out, that was the weekend of the Class of 1975 homecoming game. The weather had turned colder, so very few came that far.

In walked a family that I knew whose daughter had married well (a boy from Philadelphia, Pennsylvania) and she wanted to show him off to her hometown. That was her second mistake (subjecting him to it at all was her first.) I felt an immediate concern for him and even felt that I would like to protect him if I could. You had to be seasoned for this; you had to have been raised in such an environment to exist in it.

His wife should have prepared him. First, he was well-dressed in a tie, sports coat, and shined shoes (with strings). Next, he set out to impress everyone around him about the success of his computer business.

But this was the clincher. In his desire to fully relax in the moment, he crossed his legs and swung them out into the walking space.

Now we come to the waitress. This waitress has held that position for as long as I can remember from café to café – through the boom days and to the present. She commanded the fear and respect of every oil field hand, cowboy, gambler, or thief that has ordered his food through during all these years.

I truly thought (being a man of the world) that I and I alone knew that things were going to suddenly change in that café. I watched that waitress in the rear of the café pick up two trays to deliver just as this poor man stuck his legs out into the aisle. Now she could have picked any number of routes to go, but I knew what she would do. She bulled her neck, she widened her feet apart, she bent her legs slightly, and she charged.

As she charged by him, she hit his legs so hard that they banged against the table edge so hard that everyone heard. He was rattled, but by the time she got her pad and pencil to take their orders, he had recovered somewhat. He turned his order in first. The waitress stood in silence staring at him while he described just how he wanted his salad made and how and what he wanted on his baked potato. She wrote two words: "salad" and "tater".

The others ordered burgers and chicken fried steak like they should have. Later, when she had the orders into places on the table, she scowled at him and said "Jount dressin'?" This startled him and I could tell that he had no idea what she had said. He must have thought that if he didn't look at her that she would leave him alone.

She ran by a little later and raising her voice a little said again "Jount dressin'?" This time he scooted over a little, nearly sitting in his wife's lap. He had a bewildered look on his face and a near panic glint in his eyes.

The third time she said "I ain't gonna ask you again. Jount dressin'?" The boy completely lost it this time. He broke and ran for the door and was gone. His family finished their meal in peace and after his father-in-law finished his chicken fried steak and had picked up the bill, he passed by our table and said that the boy had had a shaky stomach ever since he had gotten there.

Early that Sunday morning as I was leaving town, the wind was blowing hard and cold from the west and, as I drove through downtown headed east, I looked back through my rearview mirror at the lonesome street and the ghost-like empty buildings. The wind was kicking up little swirls of dirt where once people had crowded together to shop or to socialize, or to talk loud or to be shy, or to just live and breathe together.

I was glad to pull upon the main highway and point the vehicle toward my Nacogdoches. My hometown has died, and I thought to myself that I don't ever want to see the same sight in my rearview mirror that I saw leaving that morning in any other town, especially Nacogdoches. But it takes all of a town's citizens working together and accepting change or it will happen. It may not happen in my time, but it will happen.

3. A REAL COWBOY IF EVER I MET ONE

They buried a real cowboy at the Old North Church Cemetery the other day. Mr. Loren F. Bouldin, late of the old cowboys' home in Stratford, Texas, was laid to rest.

It was about 1982 when I met Mr. Loren. At that time, I owned and operated a well-stocked and very western store in Nacogdoches. I had helped the customers of the moment and thought I was alone.

I looked back toward my fitting bench in the boot section where a man sat upon the bench with his back ramrod straight. His high-crown, wide-brim hat was lying in his lap. His boots, though worn, were well-shined.

I walked up and asked if I could help him. It was then that I looked into the biggest, brightest, blue eyes that I had seen on a man.

His answer was that I had already helped him. He said that he had spent about 15 minutes enjoying the wonderful smells that came from leather, saddles, boots, belts, etc. I told him that he could have all of it that he wanted – no charge, that I would even lock him in the store that night if he wanted me to.

His smile started slow, then spread until it lit up the store like a sunrise.

That's how I met Mr. Loren.

Over the next three years, I slowly learned more about him. He was born at Old Tascosa, Texas on May 9, 1898. All that is left of that wild, busy frontier town is a song and a sign by the railroad.

When he was a boy, the trail-drivers came to town to let off steam and spend their money. He watched, listened, learned and could hardly wait until he was old enough to join them. Finally, the great day came, and he earned his first day's pay as a cowboy at age 12 years. That would be about 1910.

I have in my possession a picture of him as a very handsome cowboy, setting on his favorite horse that he named Amarillo, the picture is dated 1932.

It is easily seen in looking at this picture that the thumb and one finger is all that remained on his left hand. I asked him how this happened. He said that the fingers were taken one at a time. Steers then were big, wild and fast.

You could get your fingers caught between your rope and the saddle horn, and they were gone.

Most of the big ranches were owned by the English at that time.

Mr. Loren was rightfully proud that he was picked to assist and to protect the wife of an Englishman who was visiting the ranch for an inspection.

A cowboy's most valuable possessions were his Pendleton wool bedroll and his working saddle. He showed me a copy of his will, which remained on file at ranch headquarters, stating which of his friends would get these items if he should die.

In 1940, Mr. Loren and five others were sent with a train-load of cattle to Kansas City, Missouri. They were there almost two weeks to sell the stock.

While taking in the sights, he saw (as he told it) the most beautiful girl that he had ever seen walking down the street.

He begged and pleaded until she felt so sorry for him that she married him. She was Ruth Lennox, and he took her back by train to the Matador ranch. He said that life was like living in heaven for years.

The sands of time overtook Mr. Loren and the time came that he could no longer be a top hand. Top hand or no hand, is what he said.

Why and what brought them to our country, I do not know.

Perhaps they just happened into the Old North Church, but it was an immediate love bond between the Bouldins and the wonderful caring people in the congregation.

Mr. Loren had kin living in the valley of South Texas, and he and Ruth would visit them often. In about 1969, they stopped over in Beaumont to window-shop. Loren was 71 years old then, and Ruth was 69.

They were holding hands, looking at and talking about the wonderful window displays, when a wreck in the street caused one car to slide onto the sidewalk and jerk Ruth out of Loren's grasp. It pinned her against the building and took her life.

Mr. Loren's brother, nephew, and his family wanted him to join them in the Panhandle of Texas. He felt that he just couldn't go that far away from his Ruth. He visited her often in the beautiful North Church Cemetery.

He had slowed considerably by the time I met him.

I feel very honored that towards his last days here he would venture out a couple of times a week to visit with his Ruth and come by my store for a visit, then attend church – and that was it.

He appeared unusually quiet one day and I asked how things were. He said that he had a fear of becoming a burden to his friends and neighbors, and he thought it best that he go back to the Panhandle and be with blood kin.

So, I shaped up his hat. He shined up his boots, and then he told his Ruth, me and the fine folk at North Church good-bye. Then, once again, he prepared to ride west.

The Rev. Gene Tomlin and the congregation gave him a going away party on the church grounds. Covered dishes, children playing, and Mr. Loren took center stage with the grown-ups. As he spoke, the excitement of the past built up in him and his eyes became as big and bright and blue as the ocean, and he looked young again.

They brought him back home to his Ruth the other day. The obituary will read Loren F. Bouldin, born in Tascosa, Texas, 1898, died at Coldwater Manor, Stratford, Texas, 1994. They will probably say that he was 95 years of age. But he came into the world on a beautiful spring day May 9, 1898 and left on a beautiful spring day April 2, 1994, lacking only one month of living 96 glorious years.

But wait, that is not enough. There should be a parade, there should be fine horses ridden by straight-backed cowboys. They should be leading a rider-less horse called Amarillo to honor a man who lived the life that most little boys only dream of.

Yes, they buried what may be the last of the real cowboys.

4. DEATH OF A COWBOY

Another Nacogdoches cowboy has left us. During the 1960s and 1970s Nacogdoches County had some of the best ropers in Texas.

Roy Tatum ranked among the best.

Cowboys today make their livings out in the mainstream of life. They can be plumbers, truck drivers, painters, carpenters… and many other occupations.

Roy Tatum made his living as a painter and wallpaper man. If there was a flaw in hanging wallpaper, it came down. If he painted over carpet, he did not even have to put down sheets (try getting that done today and see what happens.) This was done because his cowboy heart would not let him produce sloppy work, nor to take advantage of his fellow man.

It takes a cowboy to recognize another. Cowboy is not a thing, it is a feeling. I owned Nacogdoches Western World and supplied these people with their tack, supplies, boots, hats and clothing for years. I sat in the back of the room so that I could see my people come in.

Roy's departing ship was draped with his beautiful roping saddle. There were displayed pictures of some of his favorite times. The great bull fighter (now the Rev.) Bill Shaw officiated.

One of his five fine sons did a wonderful job of honoring his father. He also read a recent letter, written by the boy's only daughter, that brought tears to most there (including me).

A cowboy heart requires a person to provide for and live for your family. Play the game straight with your friends, and if you find a person in need, try to help them regardless of race, religion or social status.

Roy Tatum did these things. We talked one time long ago about the old Saturday Westerns that we both were raised watching. Life and rules were simple then; you had the good guys and the bad guys.

Roy was one of the good guys.

And with the words of another Roy that left us, "Happy Trails to you, until we meet again."

I hope that when you see all the old cowboy friends that have gone before, that they greet you with a good horse, good rigging, and a fine pair of boots, like I used to sell you.

5. YOUNG PEOPLE ARE GREAT

How lucky we are to live in a town where we are constantly surrounded by some of the most wonderful young people in the world.

Law enforcement will abandon personal safety to protect a vagrant just passing through town.

Paramedics will plunge into danger to save any life.

Firemen leap into an inferno to rescue.

You ask how they obtained this inner makeup of bravery and courage.

Part of the reason was that many spent their young years going into Nacogdoches Western World.

Western wear was in, and I was the owner and proprietor of a retail outlet store. But that is where my authority stopped.

When those boys and girls walked through those doors, they left the outside world and walked into a world that belonged to them.

They usually only realized that I was there when I held out my hand to take the money and put it into the register. The rest of the time I just became part of the fixtures, keeping my mouth shut and my ears and eyes open.

The years went by, and now the girls are out there doing a fine job in whatever they decided to do. Most girls have a goal, direction and motivation early, and they just go out and get it done. But the boys were different. Most seemed amazed that they could wiggle their toes and button their shirts. They would stamp around the store in Tony Lama boots, Resistol hats, Larry Mahan shirts, and a belt with their name on it. They would brag about the wild bulls and bucking horses that they were going to ride. They would say that fear was not a word that they recognized, and that they had nerves of steel.

After a time, there would come the dare to just go out to Mr. Humphrey's rodeo arena. "Well, I will sometime."

"What's wrong with now?" And, "Show us what you are made of."

Finally the moment came. Inside a wooden chute were hundreds of pounds of angry muscle. Two or three cowboys were waiting for a sit on its back.

A few never passed this point and probably went forward and found other things that helped them face life.

For most there was a sudden rush of deep fear, panic, and a feeling of "This cannot really be me, here."

Then something from deep within them took over. They felt that life without honor would be no life at all. They had passed the point of return, and there was no going back. In a day they found themselves upon the top of dynamite, and from somewhere deep within their being, the words "Turn him loose" rushed from their mouth. And for a few seconds there was no past, the future was unknown, and you and you alone were the center of the universe. Bruises and broke bones had no meaning compared to the feeling that they had of "I really did it."

And that, my friends, is why they can go every day and take care of you and me.

And to this day, and until their last day, if someone says, "Hello cowboy" they will stand straighter and feel younger and say "Yes, I am."

6. THE COURAGE TO STAY PUT

Sometime in the 1960s, each little Texas town had six to eight people who were the movers and shakers and had control. They were usually local business owners or large property owners.

They would meet in the back rooms of their local drugstores, banks, cafes, etc. and discuss their ideas, usually pertaining to how and what they could do to make themselves more money faster. After their ideas were cussed and discussed, they would send representatives to Austin. These reps would put on their shiny, fluorescent two-tone shoes, their white plastic belts, and their wide ties (usually clip-on), put leaded gasoline in their 20-foot-long cars, and head to Austin.

There, a plan was devised to murder downtown Texas. The scheme was to buy up, foreclose on or just plain take over land in a radius around these towns and call it a loop. The smallest towns would not even get a loop; the expressways would miss them completely. The larger ones would get a spur through the center. The result of this would be that those who wanted to stay in business would have to move to the loop.

It did work; most of downtown Texas is dead, dead, dead.

Now we come to our town. We have our loop and our University Drive (although our loop may be the only in existence that makes a "G"; the other property just wasn't in the right hands).

As for our University Drive, for years we had one red light at Main and University and one at University and East Austin. I don't remember what the speed limit was, but I had worn my new white hat to the mail box at Western World one morning and something went by so fast that it sucked my hat off and into the middle of University. It wasn't white anymore.

But now the tide is turning. Let me tell you about some of our people that didn't panic, didn't run, didn't sell out, stood their ground and came through standing tall.

Mr. and Mrs. David Stevens didn't move their jewelry store into University Mall where people walking by are eating popcorn or cotton candy and just trying to get in out of the heat. James and Gene Milord are still giving a good haircut at a fair price. Mr. Shaw is still stocking merchandise that the working people need. Mrs. Bright still has her store that many people in other states drive to see. The Johnsons furnish good furniture at a fair price. Mize and Schmidt's are still doing quality business as usual. Mr. J.T. Lucas and his son, Doyle, give us top quality products with good service at the price needed for top quality. I am proud for them and proud of them, for their day is here.

Mr. Sam Walton rode into these towns in the form of Wal-Mart and furnished a good product at a reasonable price; better products then offered in businesses on the loops and drives, and at a more reasonable price.

Now there is a panic rush to get back downtown and offer top quality and good friendly service again. But tough luck; it is too late; the spaces are already occupied by the people who had the courage to put character before greed.

7. A DUMB COMMERCIAL

A Texas lottery television commercial is being aired showing a grinning, laughing black man on a bulldozer destroying a beautiful green hedge and a garden statue.

Not one of my black friends thinks it funny that it is being stereotyped that black people destroy things and enjoy doing it.

Why not show a three-toothed, grinning, beer-bellied, stupid looking red-neck white man? Neither one shows anything constructive.

If the state governor knows about these things being shown, then we sure don't need him as the future president of our country.

Tonya, Mrs. Rudisill's daughter

8. WHERE THE REAL AMERICA LIES

Driving around the loop you will discover that there are numerous county road signs that show roads to travel. Turn onto any one of these, and you will be exposed to new life experiences. One of these roads is CR 1275. You can travel 6 miles down that road, turn right on a little winding tree-lined road for about half a mile, and you will come to a small but beautiful church and cemetery named the Saint's Rest.

A funeral was held there at 10 a.m. Monday, Aug. 24. The service was for a wonderful lady (Mrs. Rudisill) who had dedicated her life to caring for her family and friends. Those arriving after 9:20 found no room inside the church (not even standing room) so they quietly started gathering among the shade of the stately pines. The sun fitting its golden rays through the trees had already caused the temperature to reach nearly 90 degrees. Cars were scattered through the woods in no particular pattern. When an empty spot was found, people parked.

There were black, white, Hispanic, Oriental, elderly, babies, and handicapped – a representation of all in our county. They were neighbors, friends, and co-workers there to show their respect.

There was no complaining about the heat or the walk to get there or the discomfort of having to stand. Inside, some gave up their seats to the more needy. Outside, the young played with order among the trees while others stood in silence. There was a loving, honest, square-shouldered husband. There was a handsome, bright-eyed, grief-stricken son. A beautiful, talented, strong, dependable caring daughter held the family together and guided them through the rough storm the last two years, and did what few could do. She delivered the eulogy and told all what her mother had meant to her and what all had meant to her mother.

Her mother was formed from the seed that all those good people that rest in that, and all little country cemeteries, are made of. She lives on through the family and friends that she loves.

That is where the real America is. Those are the real Americans. Not what you see and hear on CNN news or watching "Wag the Dog" movies.

It would be a mistake to think that just because these people are honest, loyal, kind and dependable that they are also slow or ignorant. They can be gullible, they can be fooled, and they can be used, because they want to believe in their fellow man, they want to trust and help people in need. They can be lied to, yes, but my advice is to be careful in doing this. When they finally see through someone doing this, or if they are being abused, or their loved ones, friends, neighbors or strangers are in need or require assistance, their flag goes up. Many of them have baseball bats nearby. Many have Smith and Wesson's nearby. And many have both.

They know how to call 911 when an ambulance is needed, and they know how to call for that other means of transportation when it is necessary, but it doesn't have to be in a hurry to get there or to return.

9. A MATTER OF PERSPECTIVE

Recent criticism of our local judicial system reminds me of a story that a dear deceased friend told me.

His brother was and is a member of the Houston Police Department.

An educator was speaking out, wherever he could get an audience, against police brutality.

A few blocks from school one day in broad daylight, he was forced off the road by two males and a female. After being pulled from his car, he was relieved of all his jewelry and money. The female said to "check his teeth for gold". Finding none, she said "just shoot him". Others said "no, let's give him a running chance" and run he did, completely through the door of the first house he came to.

He told the police "Please get them, even if you have to use brutality."

Which leads me to wonder that if the complainers were the ones on trial, would they be so concerned about the inconvenience to potential jurors if it was their fate to be decided?

Cletus Obra "Red" Harvey

10. CARD OF THANKS – BEFORE

My father, Mr. C. O. "Red" Harvey, has recently spent an extended period of time in the Electra Hospital. I have had occasion to see a number of Texas hospitals. None compare to the expertise of your local hospital.

On behalf of my father and mother and myself, I wish to thank Dr. Huckaby and his staff for their expert care and concern for my father, Marilyn Johnson for her kindness, and Mr. Roach for his hard work in keeping the hospital clean. I also wish to thank the people from Southside Church of Christ and their preacher, Mr. Dennis Hoff, for their heartfelt concern, and many friends like Red and Glenda Thomas, the Thomas Daughertys, Mr. Leon Magness, Mr. Keith Sales, Dad's friends around the coffee table at the Dairy Queen, and the management of the Dairy Queen for sending Dad free ice cream cones.

In fact, I wish to thank all of the people of Electra for rallying around their major, LaJune Lewis, and Mr. Robb in their efforts to save my hometown.

My father has been very good to me, and has been good for the town of Electra during the 55 years that he has lived there. I, and many others, wish him a speedy recovery.

11. CARD OF THANKS – AFTER

On behalf of the family of C. O. (Red) Harvey, I want to thank the good people of Electra, Texas. The send off, for his journey to visit his mother, brothers and sisters and good friends that have gone on before him, could not have been better. I personally want to give thanks to two of your fine citizens that were somehow left off the pallbearers list – Mr. Danny Neff and Mr. Leon Magness. Let's not waste too much of our precious time on sadness. My father loved Electra and its people. He will always be around. He will be there when your beautiful trees bloom on your downtown streets, he will be there when you dedicate a newly restored building. He will be there when the Lions Club has a function. He will be there when the first baseball is tossed out each year. One of the last things that he said to me was that he hoped that "Red Thomas found his lost dog." And "Red", don't be surprised if someday you find one of those gates open that you were wanting him to open. And this to his friends around the table at the Dairy Queen: keep an empty chair there for him and he will be in it. He didn't do much talking, but he did a lot of listening.

And, if there is anything that I could do for anyone there, I will certainly try.

12. REMEMBERING NOBLE SHAW
Noble Shaw, born Dec. 1, 1909, died March 29, 1999

Very few knew him, almost all had seen him or knew of him, some did not like him, some were even afraid of him, some loved him, but everyone within his midst knew that he was there.

For over 40 years his daily routine rarely varied: Open his downtown store at a certain time, daily stocking, displaying, ordering, selling, closing and going home.

He was witty, sometimes very harsh, at times unusually kind, often strict. If he liked you, you might never know it. If he didn't, you always knew it.

Through the years, I have heard many stories told about Shaw's Department Store. One young lady recently told me she enjoyed going to the store with her daddy because Mr. Shaw kept peanuts in his pocket and would give her some.

A few years ago a friend had me meet him in a local café. He gave me a clothing order and asked me to take it to Mr. Shaw and tell him that it was an order for an uncle of mine. I took it to Mr. Shaw and told him the truth about who it was for and that the man was afraid to come in. Mr. Shaw smiled slightly and said that he would place the order.

If you tried to do the talking or ask personal questions you would get nothing, but if you remained quiet and listened you would learn.

As a boy in Quitman, Texas, he observed that people who stayed clean, neat and dressed well seemed to fare better than others. So he tried to work in white-collar jobs and invested in his clothes.

In World War II he was placed in the military police, who were required to take pride in their uniforms. He was also in the military band in Washington D.C. Discharged somewhere in California, he worked shortly at dressing windows at a department store.

I don't recall just how or why, but Mr. Mize from Nacogdoches was in touch and asked him to come to town and talk. They agreed that if at the end of 30 days either of them were dissatisfied in any way that they would still part friends.

He dressed windows until Mr. Mize started sending him back east on the trains to buy merchandise. When times got hard for people and the majority needed work clothes instead of expensive dress, he told Mr. Mize that he would like to open his own work-clothes store -- and the rest is history.

He fought the sales tax with a passion from the local level through state to the federal government.

He felt that it would not hurt the people that could pay $500 for a suit of clothes to pay $40 tax for a suit of clothes as much as the person needing a $50 pair of work boots to pay $4 tax. If a person came into his store with $50 for boots, he would write out the sales slip, and then pay the tax himself.

He was in the hospital for a week, and I offered to take him home. When I got to his room, they had just brought his lunch. He said that he would meet me in the lobby in 30 minutes. In 30 minutes, the elevator doors opened and a nurse wheeled his chair out. He was fully dressed in suit and tie, shoes shined, and hair combed. At the car, they wanted to open the door for him. He thanked them and said that he could do it.

On the way to his home he recited word for word the poem "Gunga Din"[1].

When I had a business across from his store, I would often tell people that I could perform magic by making Mr. Shaw appear around the corner of the Cox Building. At a certain time, he would come around the corner with his newspaper under one arm and his Thermos jug in his other hand.

He is gone, but I think that the wind current will change a little on that corner every morning, and I will change the words to the poem a little and say:

"He was a better man than I, Gunga Din!"

---

[1] Rudyard Kipling

13. A STORY IDEA

First, I would like to thank Mrs. Emily Taravella for being responsible for my possibly becoming rich and famous by writing a story. (She told the story of the little flat boy.)

When I was about 7 years old, my parents would drive 12 miles into the little oil field town nearest us. We would reach town usually between 10 and 11 a.m. Saturday. I would take my dime or quarter and run into the strand theater, buy my popcorn from Mrs. McSpaddin, then take my front-row seat and get ready to help Gene Autry, Hopalong Cassidy, or Buck Jones take care of the bad guys. There was always the "yellow-bellied sapsucker" and the "dirty rat", two-legged varmints who usually wore dirty black hats and had sneers on their dirty faces. I usually had a stick of gum to put in my mouth when Buck Jones did, because that was our clue that Buck was about to clean up the place.

Now to the point of this story: This past week we had a visit from my beautiful daughter and her three children, Ryan (who is fully capable of becoming anything that he wants to become), and the twins, Katy Ruth and Michael, who are in their 3s.

When they were becoming a little restless, Ryan put on a copy of a Lone Ranger movie I have. He and Michael started watching, but the little princess was still checking other things out.

I walked by and said, "Watch out for that yellow-bellied sapsucker and the dirty rat." I can only imagine what went through her head, but she immediately sat down and started watching the movie until she fell asleep.

Now this is the way that we can make a fortune. If someone out there will help me determine what animal we can use that will be kind, brave and strong, we will write stories about it coming and saving the yellow-bellied sapsucker from the dirty rat just in the nick of time.

Michael, Ryan, and Katy

14. IN DEFENSE OF FARMERS

It was written in a recent article that the farmers market was not used this year because the fruit and vegetable raisers were getting too lazy to work at it anymore.

Hold on! Wait a minute! We, the little people (known as the general public) are not going to fall for that. We all know that this location is a valuable piece of property. It could be used for another fast food outlet (those of us that have lived here a while have tried them all and need another challenge).

But my purpose is not to decide where a farmers market should be or if there should be one. I am going to defend my country friends that try hard to raise a garden or a small farm so that their families and their neighbors can have some fresh seasonal East Texas produce.

Here is the rest of the story:

Giant corporations, controlled by people that have never seen East Texas, have leased hundreds of thousands of acres of land around these country homeowners that often belonged to their parents and grandparents. These corporations lease these lands out for hunting rights at $10 per acre, taking in millions of dollars at no expense to themselves.

Hiding behind an outdated stock law, they do not have to fence their property. The only protection the little landowner has is to fence their own.

Deer fencing around a small acreage would result in a cost that would exceed the worth of their property.

This brings us to the weekend warrior. These fearless warriors sometimes consist of the types of people that either didn't go to war and shoot something or pulled every string they could to keep from going. But they do have this strong urge to shoot something. Therefore, they work hard at what the country people call deer dumping. They build up a large stock of deer on their leased lands. They then plant food in rights of way and train tracks. They build a deer blind and sit and wait for Bambi to come by. Then, with a rifle in one hand and holding up a deer head in the other, they get their picture taken beside a big pick-up truck.

Yes, this is their business, and they have their rights. But let's talk about the rights of the little people who have worked hard to plant something, either for themselves and their neighbors or to supplement their income by $1,500 to $2,000 per year. They bring local grown produce into town for city folks to buy.

But what about when you get up morning after morning and your plants have been chewed, stomped, and destroyed, and when there are 30 or 40 deer standing in your garden on flowers, and if you shoot them you could go to jail. Doesn't this mean you are too lazy to raise a crop (shame on the person who said this)?

Before deer season, some persons arm themselves with scope rifle, strap a pistol on their hip (makes them feel like Matt Dillon) and, with binoculars set out to eliminate any dogs that might chase the deer down from their feed troughs. If the small landowners' fences are knocked down by falling trees or washed away by water and their cows are into the deer feed, they can and often are hauled into court and fined.

No, my country people aren't lazy; they are just being besieged by an unjust society.

15. A LITTLE GIRL GROWS UP

Some years back (it really doesn't seem so long ago) I was preparing to start my day one morning. The sun was shining brightly and the day was clear. I looked out a front window in time to see a small girl running across the yard. The sun was shining into her hair. It was fiery red in color (I don't mean red, I mean red, red). Under it was a beautiful little face on a body about 3 feet tall. What struck me immediately was the determined look upon her face. She was a person with a goal to reach, and a purpose. Going to my car, I saw her turn into a near neighbor's house. Her mother was standing in her yard watching, so I knew she was safe, and went on with my world. I paid little attention to her through the years that followed.

One day I read where she had graduated from college, done student teaching, and received her teaching certificate.

Within the last year or so, I had the privilege of being asked to be a part of the Norman Johnson show at our local livestock show and rodeo. A beautiful red-haired woman walked up to the microphone to sing, and sing she did. I have never heard a more beautiful voice, and it is not mimicking another, it is all hers.

This past Friday, with the heavy rains coming down and amid threats of storms, a good, caring, loving family helped her load her possessions into a U-Haul. Then, with her father in the lead, and she and her mother following behind, they pointed their vehicles toward Nashville, Tennessee.

I know that while the rest of us would have worried about the weather and the fear of the unknown, she was listening to the beat of the windshield wipers and watching the rain drops, and composing music in her mind.

We will all benefit someday from this beautiful music. Yes, we will hear from her, and my word to her is "Go for it" and "Run, little girl? Run!"

Terri Jo Box

16. BUCK JONES, A TRUE HERO

Everyone came to town on Saturday in the small oilfield towns of the Texas Panhandle. The movie house was where the kids headed while the grown-ups shopped. If we got there early enough, we could sit through a good Western shoot-'um-up twice.

I had my own front row seat and Mrs. McSpradden, the owner, liked me; and if I was a little late (I came into town from the country) she saw that no one else sat in my seat.

My hero was Buck Jones. He did not curse, smoke or drink, and he did not kill folks – just winged a few. He could whip every outlaw in the bar and not get his beautiful white hat dirty. When things began to get a little out of hand and rowdy, we would all look at each other with a serious look on our faces because we all knew what old Buck was going to do next.

When we saw him pull a stick of chewing gum from his shirt pocket (I usually saw him first) and put it in his mouth, we all knew that the villains had had it.

When it was all over, the bar looked as if it had been hit by a tornado, and the outlaws were carted off to jail.

We did not get to keep Buck long. He died the hero we all knew he was. He had assisted three people out of the flames and had returned for more, when he and 500 people perished in the Boston fire of the Coconut

Grove Night Club in 1942.

To this very day, I can still tell, from what Buck taught me, whether or not someone is a good guy or a bad guy just by sizing them up.

17. THE TELEVISION GUIDE

The "theys" are at it again. Forget for awhile now the murders, the car wrecks, and the politicians questioning the ancestry of their opponent.

We all have a more pressing problem. The "theys" are messing with our TV guide. Two weeks ago we opened our Sunday papers and searched even more frantically than usual for the most important thing in the paper.

What we found was a conglomeration of words and letters. People panicked. Sheriff Joe Evans' prisoners raised their cups on the bars, people in nursing homes refused to eat. At least one person had to be placed under oxygen.

It has to be a plot of the "theys" coming out of Lufkin or Houston to bring Nacogdoches to its knees. The life-line to what's happening, who is doing what, and what needs to be done in Nacogdoches is the "Norman Johnson Show". It is not even listed.

The people responsible for this mess should be apprehended, punished, and given a job counting rubber bands.

Editor's note: "They" didn't do it, we did. The local listings for Channel 21 should be back in today's television guide. See Ernie Murray's column for an explanation of why the listings format was changed.

18. REMEMBERING DR. CRAVENS

Dr. John Nathan Cravens Sr. has left us. He has gone on to new adventures. But he will remain in the memories of hundreds and hundreds of long ago ex-college students distributed throughout the world.

In a small college in the very forgettable town of Wichita Falls, Texas, many of us had just been discharged from the service in what was called the Korean conflict. Some of us were working the oil fields at night and going to classes on the GI Bill in the day. It was hard to hold our attention, but one man made the difference.

My mind has instant recall of rushing to attend a history class. A tall man would always be standing at the chalkboard, always flashing a wonderful smile, eager to begin. Students were also eager to be seated.

He would raise his long arm and begin to weave a beautiful story of our history.

If I am fortunate enough to be on this earth as long as he was, I will always be the student, and he (by past examples set) will remain the teacher.

19. CLIFFORD MARTIN WOULD NEVER BOW DOWN

The scene is a little school in the Panhandle of Texas. Maximum enrollment from 1st through 12th grade was 135 little souls. The time was 1944 and our country was at war.

The characters were about 13 to 15 sixth-grade students. Their teacher, Mrs. Turkey. The principal and superintendent, Mr. Newcome. The main character (and I am proud of him to this day) was a fellow student and comrade-at-arms, Clifford Martin. (The only real names used will be myself and Clifford Martin. Why? Because after 40 years, I am still scared of these people; and they probably have been dead for 20 years.)

It was a wonderful school building, with long windows in every room with a full view of the outside world. In retrospect, I know now that Mrs. Turkey was probably a fine lady and meant well for all of our poor little ignorant souls.

Our day might be going quite well until Mrs. Turkey accidentally screeched the chalk on the blackboard. We all knew that this was it.

We had learned to have our heads bowed and our eyes closed, before ordered to do so. The ranting and raving about the Lord would begin. Sometimes points were emphasized with the blows of a ruler upon her desk. She would never get far into her ravings when she would scream,

"Clifford Martin, bow your head or go to Newcome's office!"

Clifford, appearing to be unruffled, would already be on his feet and headed out the door, cool in the line of fire, while our nerves were always frayed and shaken.

Now, as I mentioned, World War II was on but they wouldn't take Newcome because he had feet that were about two inches wide and one and one-half foot long.

He had to have special mail order shoes and he would make all our lives as miserable as possible if a newly ordered pair wasn't delivered on time. I personally wrote the president of the United States, Mr. Franklin Delano Roosevelt, a letter asking him (begging him) to put this man in the Army, and I would bale hay and cut wheat for money to personally pay for his shoes. I will never forgive Roosevelt for not answering my letter.

Newcome would order Clifford to bend over his desk for his whipping. Clifford would refuse and took his medicine standing straight up. Clifford's father was on the school board, and a note was pinned to Clifford's overalls to be carried home. It outlined his conduct. We all knew that things had gone a little rough on the boy, because he would look a little frayed around the edges the next day. But he was always smiling and showing us a new marble, frog, or turtle.

When asked why he wouldn't cooperate, his answer was that Mrs. Turkey had to be cheating and raising her head, or she would not have caught him. He also said that none of us were going to get by with shooting him with a paper wad, because he was watching us.

I lost track of Clifford Martin in the early fifties. Although I have never read nor seen on TV where a Clifford Martin won a Nobel Prize, neither have I heard where a Clifford Martin became a mass murderer. I do know that wherever Clifford is today, he has never bowed and he has never bent over unless he wanted to do so.

I will always believe that if we'd had five minutes per day of silent prayer to let us sort out our own thoughts and just let Clifford and the Lord work out their own problems with each other, it would have been much easier on us all.

20. P & Z IN GOOD HANDS

One Monday, the 18th, at 3:30 p.m., I attended the regular meeting of the session of the city planning and zoning commission. There were two reasons for my attending. One was my interest and concern about what goes on in our downtown and two, I wanted to see just what a planning and zoning commission does.

The issue at hand was to answer a request for permit to operate a private club at 510 East Main Street. We were each handed a card that stated:

1. Do you want to speak for the issue?
2. Do you want to speak against the issue?
3. Are you a spectator?

I signed mine spectator.

This is what I learned as a spectator. The persons asking for the permit have operated two clubs in Nacogdoches for a number of years. They are very professional and have cooperated with the city in every way. Their businesses have been an asset to Nacogdoches. They are decent, hardworking, respected people who have nothing but good will towards our town. Their backers were some of the finest. Those in opposition were also some of our best and finest people.

Their arguments were equally sound. That's why I marked spectator, because I am not qualified. I am a face reader. I watched the faces on the panel that has to do the judging.

I left there satisfied that no matter how this issue is decided, that after all these years, Nacogdoches has a panel of people that will weigh the issues or the good of our downtown and will decide without any thought of personal gains.

Their chairperson is a very capable young lady, whom I watched (with only a glass window and a street between us) put in long hard hours starting her own business. And knowing all along that customers would have a difficult time getting to her business. I left there knowing that the flame has been lit for the re-birth of downtown Nacogdoches and that the planning and zoning of it is in capable hands.

21. A CLASS ACT DOWNTOWN

The ladies of Nacogdoches have a class act at their disposal, right here in their hometown. They don't have to take bus tours, plan vacations, etc. just to see one. In fact, I have spent time in many of the small Texas towns that attract tourists: Jefferson, Marshall, and Fredericksburg. Even San Antonio and our Louisiana neighbor, Natchitoches, don't have one.

Most towns have always had a place where men could go to visit over a cup of coffee, but the women have had to meet in their homes.

Furnished with fine antiques, there is a beautiful counter and stools, a number of priceless tables and chairs, set with china and linen, and wonderful smells of gourmet coffees and teas. As I said, a first-class act – with vision, know-how and just plain nerve to try it. Mrs. Phyllis Anderson and Mrs. Marilynn Sparks, along with the help of Mr. John Schmidt, have put it together at the downtown Schmidt's store.

They are not equipped for crowds. With pre-arrangement, your ladies clubs, newcomers, garden clubs, or just a few friends, can lunch there and be treated royally.

22. IMPRESSED WITH JP COURT

Recently I was asked by the mother of a teen-aged son to accompany her son to the court of Precinct 3 as a character witness.

The court was handled smoothly and duly. No foul language was permitted, no outbursts of anger or accusations on either side allowed. Each side had equal opportunity to present their case. No hearsay was allowed; proof had to be presented. The young man that I stood with admitted that he had been wrong; so he was allowed to return to school; however, he was advised by Judge Mike Worsham what he could expect should his behavior continue.

Another young man blamed his school, blamed his family, blamed the weather, blamed everything and everybody but himself, and when he leaned on the judge's bench, he was advised to stand erect in the courtroom. Then he was ordered to perform some work days and follow a schedule for a period of time.

Judge Worsham's record in this position indicates that he is quite capable of the highest performances of his duties.

23. A WORLD WAR II MUSEUM

The people of the Texas Panhandle town of Pampa are building a museum to honor the people that fought for their country in World War II.

My family is in the process of cleaning my Uncle Frank's uniform, shining his brass, some medals, and other mementos that he had, which they will donate to his museum.

My Uncle Frank and two brothers left the dust bowls of Oklahoma in the late 1920s by hopping a train and going to the Texas Panhandle to an oil boom. Later they brought their mother and two sisters and a brother to join them. Uncle Frank was the only one that had to go "over there".

He sent back to my mother "Evening in Paris" perfume from France. He mailed me a rabbit fur cap with a Nazi swastika on it and a gas mask.

My family lived at the time in a small (but clean) shotgun house about 9 miles from the nearest community. At every opportunity when I was freed by a school bus, I would saddle my horse and escape to a world of my own. There my imagination would go to work and I would help my Uncle Frank and America all I could.

I didn't dig fox holes because my house might fall in, so my mind went to work. I would climb out of my fox holes (I was always the leader), would stand straight under strong enemy fire. I would motion my men to follow me into battle. I didn't die easy and it took a machine gun to bring me down. I would kick. I would call for water and the medics. This could go on for long periods of time, and on those times that I did die, all my men would gather around me and I would order them to leave me and wipe out those Nazis. My old horse would watch me until I was a goner, then would start eating grass.

Sometimes I would return a hero, by train, wounded and on crutches – full uniform and medals. The band would play. Boys would stand in envy; the girls would help me off.

Somehow the glory stopped when the Korean War came along and I saw firsthand the reality of war.

My Uncle Frank was the family hero. He drove a truck all over Europe. And probably didn't even kill anyone.

But he did get to drive General Patton's jeep around for awhile, and he served his country honorably.

He has a safety award from Shell Oil Company, stating that he worked 42 years without injury to himself or his fellow workers.

Then he died and his wife, my beautiful Aunt Gladys, fell to the horrors of arthritis and is in a nursing home somewhere in Oklahoma. I say I will visit her and tell her how much I loved her, but I probably won't.

We should get together a museum here for our heroes. So that they won't be forgotten. We had many that did not return from over there. Both white and black.

Some whites that come to mind were Bill Bobo, Fred Buckner, Burleson Conley, Joe Hargis, Loarn Weems, and the list goes on and on. Some of the black men were L. T. White and Willie T. White, brothers. Many of our black soldiers were heavily decorated and some died as the result of war.

Think about it.

24. SOUND OFF (1)

This is in regard to the derogatory remark made about Marion Upshaw's radio show. Upshaw's radio program was aired at an inconvenient time of the day for us, so we cannot make a judgment on it, but we do know the man. He was an excellent educator, a wonderful father, and a fine, law-abiding citizen. Anyone making derogatory remarks about him should at least have the courage to sign his or her name.

25. SOUND OFF (2)

This is for my friend and yours – Cletus Harvey:

Man, you have outdone yourself on the death of a small town. This is the best thing I have read in the daily paper in the last 40 years. If you will go east and spend some time you may come up with another story on a small dead town called San Augustine. Man, give it a try. I would like to hear another one.

Sgt. York

26. NURSES ARE HEROES

The day had been a fine day, spent in our beautiful town surrounded by our wonderful people.

It was coming to a close, time for a bath and pajamas, and a little reading. I did not make it to the reading part. I have always heard of the hard mule kick; well, I got mine.

My wife called 911 and in minutes I stepped out into the strong arms of two knights in shining armor. My chariot of silver with the flashing lights awaited me. Strapping me in, they immediately began making me secure, checking vital signs and recording information. First stop, emergency room. Efficiency was everywhere there also; prompt attention, asking questions, looking for any way to ease their patient's concerns. Then the tests to define the problem. Cause found, they advised me as to what had to be done, got my consent, and told me that I would be asleep for awhile. My next knowledge of the world was of the nurse following the doctor's orders, loading the IVs, setting the charts, and giving their patient their absolute attention.

They are the everyday heroes out there. They give their best to every patient. And work under some conditions that I could not have imagined.

My thanks to all those heroes, the paramedics, the emergency room people, the x-ray staff, the nurses and their assistants, and the wonderful doctors. I can only hope that when they do get to return home, they are appreciated by the people that live with them and that they, in turn, realize that they are heroes.

I have heard the term "shop around for your health needs". I am still here to tell you now that when you get that kick and you are yelling Lordy, Lordy, why me, it will be our local heroes who will do their best to save your life.

The nine days were finally over and as they were chairing me out, the nurses all looked up to say goodbye and then turned back to their never-ending task of saving some other poor soul.

Riding to the hospital, I remember thinking of all that I needed to do. We all have our But I's, But I woulda, But I should, But I coulda. I was told that I came within a few hours of using up all my But I's. And if I had, they would have just disappeared into a vapor, and the only thing left of my existence would be what was left in the minds of people who knew me.

Cletus Obra "Red" Harvey and Ethna Genet Harvey

27. HIS MOTHER'S STORY

Miss Idabel Oklahoma of 1930 was my mother.

My grandfather had 40 acres of land and worked in a sawmill while trying to make a living for five sons and three daughters. He burned his candle out early and died.

The two older sons heard of the oil boom in Borger, Texas, hopped a freight train and painfully made their way to the Texas Panhandle. After finding jobs and getting money to send back, one brother went back to Idabel and brought back his mother, three brothers, and two sisters. The oldest sister had already made it to California. My mother was one of the two girls, and this is where I come into the picture.

My father was the second oldest of a large family that had settled west of Fort Worth, Texas. Their father had also died, and times were hard. His brother had found work in Borger and sent for him. Both mailed money back to support the others.

My mother had been there but a short time when she saw this tall thin, red-headed, freckle-faced boy in a baseball uniform throwing rocks at tin cans placed on a fence, and that was that.

Major oil companies then had their own ball teams and 18-year-old C. O. "Red" Harvey had a fast ball.

I was raised hearing the story of "The old Indian in Oklahoma". My grandfather had befriended an old Indian!

Most every day when the Genet children got out of school, he was waiting to see that they arrived home safely.

This embarrassed my mother, as she felt that she needed no supervision, and besides, he smelled of wood smoke.

The years flew by, and after spending 65 years together, "Red" died.

My mother put up a brave fight to become interested in life, but it was no use. She missed her red-haired ball player.

When I received the call from the wonderful little hospital that operated in a small Texas town that she had died, it took me seven hours to drive there, and of course her room had been cleared "except for personals".

The room was the same one that my father had died in.

The nurse said that she had just checked on her and stepped out of the room for a short time – and she was gone.

Now, I know the rest of the story. The "old Indian" was just waiting for his chance to come for her, and I will always believe that I sensed the faint smell of wood smoke in that room.

"Red" and Ethna Harvey

Charles Haney and Cletus Harvey

28. A LEADER OF MEN IS GONE

Well, it's been a year since the big man died. He knew that he was dying, but he was too private and dignified to want other people to know it.

He told me that he didn't want me to write anything about him when he was gone. I did not want to lie, so I told him I probably couldn't think of anything good anyway. He said "I mean it Hoss!" I never asked him why he called me that, although I liked it. I told him I would wait a year and by then all his enemies would know it anyway. Well, the year is here.

Charles Wesley Haney was born in Houston. The Haneys had left Appleby during the 1930s in an attempt to escape poverty. His father was assistant police chief in Houston during some of its roughest years, leaving the big man with a strong feeling about law and order. Out of high school and into police school, he was placed as a motorcycle officer. But when he and a friend were reported for standing in the seat riding down South Main, his father put him to walking a beat.

This didn't quite excite him, so he quit, went to Texas A&M, and then enrolled in the military. From there he went to Army investigation, then back to Houston working for the district attorney's office. Then, using his dynamic personality, he entered the pipeline business right away and worked in almost every state in the Union, finally ending up as district manager in charge of 17 eastern states.

He had a photographic memory and it was not necessary for me to use a library because answers were just a phone call away.

He was a leader of men. He respected the rights of his fellow man. He didn't use foul language because he was afraid his long-dead mother might find it out. He was my living answer to a John Wayne, and he wasn't acting. Near the end, he became bored and would try to entertain himself. Regardless of how deep I would try to make my voice when answering the phone, he would call out my wife's name and ask to speak to Cletus. Then he would laugh.

He would try to pay our way out of a café with his library card. He would tell the waiter or waitress at a small place that we had just talked to a bus load of old folks and they were intending to eat there in a hurry. Oh, I was so embarrassed at times!

He cut me a tape of my favorite country songs and personally announced the title and the name of the singer of each song. I thought "Does he think that I am too dumb to know this?" Well, I found that tape the other day and I have already made three copies, just in case I break one. His strong clear voice comes out, and it is comforting.

He is gone, he won't be back, and that's it. But the would'ves, should'ves, could'ves that I could have done for and with him make me be nicer to the friends that I have left.

My close friends are passing on, and I find myself afraid to make new ones. It hurts me too much when you lose them.

But as Bob Hope said, "Thanks for the memories!"

29. WORSHAM'S RETIREMENT

He first walked into Nacogdoches Western World in the mid-1970s. At the time, he was a deputy under Sheriff John Lightfoot. It has always been my opinion that a true law enforcement officer comes into this world wanting to be one.

I have never asked the judge if that is true, but I am sure that it is so with him, because it cannot be the money. It seems that we have never learned to compensate those in society whom we need the most – law enforcement, firemen, medical help, etc.

He walked, talked and dressed the part of a lawman, and through the years he has served the people who depended on him with fairness, compassion, honesty and devotion to the law.

We all recognize that we will be losers as he leaves his job, but we wish him the very best.

Judge, I tried to pass the hat to buy you a beautiful registered quarter horse, but everyone is hollering about gas prices. I understand that you have two fine horses, so just enjoy them until times get better, and I will try again.

30. SHOWTIME

It was pacemaker time – me at 8:00 a.m. on a Thursday at Mother Francis hospital in Tyler Texas. Over by 10:00 a.m., I was wheeled to my room and was told I would be home on Friday morning.

8:00 a.m. Friday morning dismissal tests were performed. It was found that a wire had slipped and that I would have to stay another day and have more surgery.

Looking out the window at a coming storm I was just about at the bottom of the barrel.

Now here is what happened next…

I have some dear friends that have gone on to the better place ahead of me. The "Big Man", Mr. Charlie Haney, said that "Old Hoss needs some help!" Mr. Ron Franklin Holmes (an ex Texas Ranger) said "How can we help Cletus?" Mr. George Grimes said "Let's do something for Cletus because we don't want him up here yet causing trouble!"

They talked it over with the One in charge of us all.

At 10:00 a.m. lightning struck outside my window, knocking out power at the hospital. Emergency power kicked in and I was wheeled to surgery. I was on my way home by 1:00 p.m.

Thanks boys! I will wait a while before I come to start causing you trouble.

31. WORLD'S GREATEST GUARDIAN
By Ryan Christopher Bruning

I think my grandfather, Cletus Sylvester Harvey, is the greatest of my relatives because he knows some of the coolest stories of the old west. Cletus Sylvester Harvey is my mom's father and I call him Pawpaw. He used to own a store in Nacogdoches, Texas called Nacogdoches Western World. His store sold cowboy hats, boots, saddles, belts, and any other kind of cowboy item you can think of (but not the horse or cow). He also had a store in the historic downtown area called Cletus' Corner. There he sold special coffees (this was even before there were Starbucks!). All the people would come in, have coffee and a snack and visit with my Pawpaw.

I like going over to his house because he has the coolest things. He has an old pistol, a big backyard, Chinese checkers, a giant picture room, and a whole series of the TV show "The Lone Ranger". He and I like playing tricks on my mom by burying big 5 gallon containers of coins in his backyard. Only he and I know where they are buried and I'm not telling! These are just a few reasons why I think he is the greatest!

Susan Harvey and Brad Harvey

32. A LETTER TO HER DADDY
By Susan Harvey Bruning

Daddy,

This room with all your things is an empty shell without you. I know that you hated being in that hospital bed but I'm amazed how your presence of being a strong man never left you. I hope you know that in my eyes you could never change that… certainly no hospital gown, wheelchair or any medical apparatus.

I love you with all my heart,
Your Suzi

33. REQUIEM FOR BUCKSHOT

Buckshot Reynolds (I am sure that he had a first name, but I never knew it) and I were the only oil field brats in a North Texas farming community. Our fathers pumped shallow leases. It was eight miles north of the town of Vernon.

Plowed fields were laid out in sections, with dirt roads making a square. One mile east was the Waggoner ranch land, horses, cows, cowboys and freedom. That's where Buckshot and I stayed. The farm boys had to work after school. We felt sorry for them, but there was nothing we could do to help them. We both had horses and were on them shortly after the school bus stopped.

Buckshot heard of a rodeo nearby, and we both entered. He was small and rode a bull. I was tall with long legs, so I rode a bareback bronc.

That started it.

He would hear of a show and away we went, always leaving early so if the old pickup we kept patched up quit on us Buckshot would grab his bull rope, I would grab my rigging and we would stick out our thumbs and hitch a ride.

Buckshot had a wild streak. He would talk of Montana and Wyoming. He was never a bad boy – he would never lie, be dishonest or disrespectful, but he would cause a little trouble – like dancing with some tough guy's girl at a rodeo dance or staying on the bus after it reached school and sleeping until a recess or the lunch bell woke him.

Once, he cut the weight on the stage curtain shortly after the play had started.

I was a fair bronc rider, but Buckshot was a natural bull rider. He could have been a champion.

In those days, bull riding came in the middle of a show. (Today it's last because it is a crowd-pleaser and holds their attention.) He was on the last of the bulls, and I was on the chute getting ready to be the first of the bronc riders.

I turned just in time to see the head of a very large beast meet the head of a very small cowboy.

I, the crowd, the clowns, and the ambulance drivers all knew that Buckshot was gone before he hit the ground. Shortly after, my father transferred to oil field ranch country, and I had a new environment. I would try a ride occasionally to show those other oil field boys how tough I was, but my heart was not in it.

Months, and even years, go by now without my thinking about Buckshot. But when I do, I remember the look of pure satisfaction he would have on his face when he would ease down on a bull, and that special wild yell he would give when he told them to "turn him loose".

I think of the life he missed, the family he didn't raise, the friends he didn't make, the satisfaction of a job that he never got to enjoy.

But he also missed the possibility of growing old, useless and unwanted, missed the age of the efforts to keep a person going (at all cost) with the help of medication and pain pills.

And I wonder whether maybe, just maybe, if Buckshot had known the risk, would he still have chosen that five or six seconds of glory.

34. A HONEY OF A CAR

At 11 a.m. on Oct. 28, 2008, I was stopped at a light at University Drive and Park Street. I looked down at my mileage. It read 177,777.7. The light changed and in a split second the mileage changed. That moment in time will never happen again. Coincidence maybe.

Now I will tell you about my beautiful white Lincoln Towncar named Rocinante, after Don Quixote's horse. Now, I am going to say this (and I will watch your faces for telltale signs that you are thinking that you suspected as much) – I talk to Rocinante. It had 29 miles on it when I first got behind its wheel. For five or six years, miles were logged spending eight- to twelve-hour days traveling to the Texas Panhandle to perform family obligations around Dallas through Fort Worth, and through Dallas around Fort Worth. We tried every road there was to get to the West from Nacogdoches, at least twice or more per month, in all kinds of weather.

Never once did Rocinante falter. I had to hold it back (police still hide behind road signs west of Fort Worth).

And sometimes it seemed to drive itself. It served as a windbreak while standing in some small High Plains cemetery. It was a lifesaver with its air conditioner in August.

Through the years, it has had the best of oil, the best of gasoline.

There has never been a shop's touch placed on it except for Tipton Ford in Nacogdoches – Mr. Coats, Mrs. Gresham, Mr. SGT. Preston, and many others who give you their attention as soon as you arrive. Probably the best in the business. Auto bailout – forget it. Just build a good automobile, treat it right, and let the right people repair it.

Sheriff Joe Evans

35. THE SHERIFF'S A GOOD MAN

I was in business in Nacogdoches County for 17 years. One of my customers was a young highway patrol officer. He was always well groomed and could have been the person on a recruiting poster. His manners were excellent and he captured the admiration of many of the young people passing through my store. Some of them went on to seek a career in law enforcement themselves because of him. He could have easily moved on in his career to higher paying and more rewarding jobs.

Because he wanted to make a mark in history as being a great sheriff in one of the oldest counties in Texas, he discussed running for office with his lovely and supportive family. He ran and won and we know the rest.

There were factions that immediately set out to control him. I ask why. What do they have to gain?

Some say he has to play politics and get along.

Well, he doesn't have to do squat; his job description is banged out by the State of Texas. He knows his job quite well. At the time of his election, there were very few in Texas that had more instruction in law enforcement than he.

Our job is to supply the money for him to protect us.

He was recently criticized for using inmates to help some needy people to repair their roads.

There are many inmates sitting in our prisons that are wanting a chance to redeem themselves. They have not harmed us nearly as much as some legitimate businessmen that are not in jail. The sheriff can spend 15 minutes with a man and tell whether or not he is worthy.

So let's find out why he has these obstacles thrown before him.

Or vote him out and let him get on with his life in peace. If you elect a "yes man" in his place, I am going to do my best to protect mine and his, and some other good people that I know who believe in him. And when the time comes that you say "Oh look at what happened to me", you can just stand there and whistle Dixie.

36. THE TALE OF "OLD TUFFY"

The winters in the Texas Panhandle during the 1940s and early 1950s could get very cold.

One cold morning with snow covering the ground, I trudged to the barn to feed my horse and to break the ice in the water trough.

The ground under the trough was frozen, of course, but it was free of snow, and that's where I found him. The ugliest dog I had ever seen. He had fresh cuts all over; even his ears looked like they had been chewed on. The cowboys said that he looked like the coyote had eaten on him and that he was probably a goner. I treated his cuts, wrapped him in saddle blankets, fed him when he would eat, and by spring he became a holy terror.

He became a Kato, like that man who worked for Peter Sellers in the movie "Pink Panther". He would crouch and catch me off guard and then attack. He would growl and grab my trouser leg and chew on the tops of my boots. He would not stop until he had me down and I was perfectly still, then he'd go find something else to terrorize.

He would wait for me to get off the school bus, beat me to the barn, and when I would nearly get my horse saddled he would bite at the horse's legs and get the horse, the cows, the pigs, the chickens, every living thing in sight all worked up. I named him "Old Tuffy" and during the winters of 1946, 1947 and 1948, he was my best friend.

He had one weakness. He could hear a coyote howl before I could, and his ears would perk up, he would growl, and be off to do battle.

I would be in bed with covers piled high with just my ears and nose out, raise my window an inch or two, listen to the howls and know that Old Tuffy was out there trying to hold his own.

Often, he would drag in, and I would patch him up again. The men said that if I wanted to keep him, I had better chain the fool up at night. I did one night, and the next morning he would not look at me. It was as if he wanted nothing more to do with me. I could not stand this, and never chained him again.

One cold night in 1948, with a full moon shining, I heard a pack off in the distance. The next day, there was no Old Tuffy. I rode the pasture for days looking for him, with no luck. The cowboys said he had chased them further than I thought and that they had ganged up on him.

But I had my own thoughts on that subject.

I think that Old Tuffy whipped the whole bunch and that he had decided "I will just run this outfit now."

During the rest of the winter of '48, when I would hear the howls, it seemed that I could hear a bark and a growl among them.

37. A POEM
By Bubba Dietz

    My Friend

If in need – there's a friend I could call
No questions – he'd be there in no time at all
Most don't know the good he's done in the past
I do – 'cause we're both molded from the same cowboy cast
Always true to his word
Said it in a way clearly understood
Good friend – better than half my life
Who can say that this day and time?
I want to give him praise before he's put to rest
Thru the years – friends I've made – he's truly among the best
I love you for what and who you are
To me you will always wear that shining star

    Love ya Cletus,
    Bubba

38. LOLA BERRY, A TRUE LADY

Lady Lola Reese Berry, born July 13, 1912, died Sept. 4, 2008

Mrs. Lola Berry was raised in the Garrison community. But she was bused (a bus being a truck with side boards and row of seats nailed to each side) to Timpson to high school.

At age 16 she could ride a bus (some kind) from Garrison to Appleby for one dime. Then she could go from Appleby to Nacogdoches for another dime.

Her first paying job was on Shawnee Street. She and another lady made tamales for the tamale man. He would then load his cart and push it to the square downtown and sell his wares.

She would also assist Dr. Steven Tucker when he would treat the black people, either in school, church or funeral home.

She then started working in the homes of white people. Her favorite was the Jones family, who lived in the gingerbread house that still stands near the hotel. She prepared the food, cleaned the home and organized the children's activities – working from early morning until late afternoon – walking both ways on Orton Hill.

When and where she met Mr. Berry I don't know. He became a soldier in World War II and when he got out they moved to Detroit.

Her time there she considered to be the best part of her life. She worked for a family of means who had three small children when she started, a daughter and two sons.

She raised them. They were told by their parents when they wanted something to ask Lola and, until the day she died, they still looked to her as a mother.

Her husband died, and she moved into a high-rise apartment. Looking out her window one morning, she saw some vandals stripping an expensive automobile. One saw her and pointed at her. She came back to Nacogdoches.

Lady Lola worked for people but was never a hired hand. She quickly became part of the family, and they were devastated if she had to leave. She paid her own bills, lived alone, and drove her own car until her last two weeks. Even after breaking both wrists, she would accept just a little help until she could get back to work.

I called her Lady Lola and meant every word of it. She had a walk that showed pride and confidence. I would tell people "you may get close to the Lola walk, but you will not copy it."

So go on your journey, Lady Lola, to a place where there is not racism, no prejudice, and no seeing the world in black and white.

And you, Lady Lola, do not have to take a back seat to anyone when you walk with that Lola walk to receive your crown.

39. WHY DIDN'T I BE MORE NEIGHBORLY BEFORE IT WAS TOO LATE?

When I moved into this neighborhood 22 years ago, I knew no one and no one knew me.

There was a man (later dubbed "the old-timer") at the house across the street. His two-car garage had been converted into a well-organized shop on one side with his car on the other. A Hunter fan had been installed in the ceiling. There were two lawn chairs on the floor. The one that he used had a flat board across the seat with a thin cushion in it; the other was just a simple lawn chair.

That first day I wanted to be neighborly, so I looked for a chance to catch his eye so that I could wave. It didn't happen, so I settled in and forgot about him. Later, after getting to know others around me, I learned that he and his wife had returned here to the land of their roots after spending their productive years somewhere in California – he as a machinist and she as a school teacher.

Days and years went by with myself and the old-timer doing yard work – sometimes as close as 20 feet apart – without speaking.

Some 10 years went by and one day he saw me standing on the air conditioning unit, reaching as high as possible to do some painting on the house. He yelled across and said that he had "an extension ladder if you want to borrow it". This was going to be the big breakthrough; we were going to be buddies. I extended the ladder out as far as possible, placed it against the house, got my bucket and brush, and climbed to the eaves of the house. The ladder slipped – not its fault, but mine – and as I went by the air unit it caught my shoulder and jerked it out of place. The old-timer and another neighbor gathered up what they could of me and sent me off to the emergency room where Dr. Pennington and Dr. Jorgenson discussed the possibility of my making it through life with one arm stuck in the air, then decided to put my shoulder back in place.

I didn't ever borrow from him again because I knew that he thought this fool might kill himself with his screwdriver and he would go to jail. So, the next few years went by with only a wave and nod of recognition between us.

Somewhere in those years, he decided that he wanted to make some mad money, as his wife told it. So, he bought a tractor and some mowing equipment and contracted to mow three or four graveyards. He kept his car serviced and clean. Often he would dress in his "come catch me" hat (as he called it), shirt, tie, dress trousers, suspenders, shined shoes – and he and his wife would drive to Shreveport, Madisonville, Tyler or Longview just to eat lunch and return.

But then his wife died and he didn't care about mad money anymore. He would spend his days in his shop with the garage doors open, fan going and setting in his chair watching the street so as not to miss any activity that might be going on.

Finally, the day nurses started coming some during the week, but he wouldn't go for Meals on Wheels. He would dress and go to the hospitals, senior citizens center, or Brookshire Bros. for his food. I didn't get too chummy with him because time spent with him might cut into my very, very important time.

The day nurses thought that he needed attention the other day – and they were right. An ambulance was called and he was taken to the hospital. In a few days, it was decided that he would not be able to live at home again, so he was taken to the nursing home. He did not like the nursing home; so in less than 12 hours he just died. Myself and all my neighbors said "Oh, what a shame."

But you know what? I still peek out my window and wish I could see those garage doors go up, that I would see his car back out with him behind the wheel with his little "come catch me" hat on or see him resting in his chair with his work gloves on his knee and wiping sweat with his bandana.

Why didn't I say hello more? Why didn't I walk over there and sit in that other lawn chair and say "Hello neighbor. I like the comfort of having you over here and what can I do to help your life?"

Well, I didn't and now I never can, and I am certainly not a better person for it.

40. TAKE CARE OF MR. SMOOTH

One night 44 years ago, I took a walk down a nature trail along the San Antonio River. There were warnings out that you should not walk alone, that you might be mugged and robbed, and that the city would not be responsible.

As a new Army draft inductee, nothing scared me as much as what might be ahead, so I walked anyway.

Today, there are beautiful shops and restaurants that line both sides of this river, where thousands can relax and experience a pleasant, enjoyable drop back into a slower pace in life. It has brought billions of dollars into the city of San Antonio.

Today, in Nacogdoches, we have a nature trail along Lanana Creek that Dr. Abernethy and a few wonderful hard-working, civic-minded people have supplied for us all to use. It is a much better trail than the one I walked so many years ago.

Soon our new city commissions are going to be faced with their first major decision.

There has been a request by a business to get a beer license. The business is located on Park Street along the creek. There are good people who live on the west side of the creek and they fear they might get noise pollution.

"Well, tough luck." When the powers that be extended that part of Park Street, the good people in their homes did not know whether they would wake up with a rendering plant or a toxic dump in their yards, but no one listened to them.

Now, the license to sell drinks is not the problem. San Antonio would not be where it is without the sale of spirits. There are some outstanding people that enjoy a social drink. Some of my best friends are drunks, but they do not impose their condition upon someone else.

Now, to what our new commissioners are facing. The planning and zoning committee had no choice but to give their approval, because it has been commercially joined.

One day last week, I thought that I would look at the operation myself. I might want to recommend it to our tourists and visitors.

Well, here it is: A large screened-in area put together with a few boards and screen. Wood tables already covered with dirty words in color, mostly about what someone would like to do with someone's daughters. There were paper cups sitting around half-filled with some kind of stale liquids and cigarette butts, and banners from every beer company available were hanging anywhere they could hang.

Now, here is what we have: (I am going to eliminate girls from this criticism, because girls today usually have a purpose and direction in life and are working toward it. We all know about "Bubba", so we don't have to explain him.)

That brings us to "Mr. Smooth".

He comes into our institution of higher learning from another region. His parents are usually fortunate enough to have more than average income. They send him away mainly because they can't stand him either, but they send him away with money to spend. He spends his day bluffing his way by hook or crook. He picks up a few followers who like his crudeness, his vulgarity, and his lack of respect for his fellow man. He is the kind that, if his parents should cut back on his money supply or in any way annoy him, he would seek a safe haven where he could rush into (down quiet little Park Street), gobble down some catfish and hushpuppies, slosh down a few beers, then sit back, talk vulgar, write a few dirty words, and get a few laughs from others just like him. Then he staggers down our nature trail to throw a few cans, hushpuppies and whatever else at the people trying to walk the creek.

Commissioners, San Antonio did some long-range planning about their river. You need to think hard about our creek.

So, let them have their license, lay down strict rules and regulations and enforce them. Give the owner full cooperation and let him hire a big burly bouncer with a ball bat and when "Mr. Smooth" gets out of line and reaches for his car keys (to spin out on little Park Street, possibly in the path of little Johnny and Jane on the way to or from school), let him tap him on the knuckles or the side of the head, drag him out to Park Street, and let our local law cart him away.

41. END OF THE TRAIL?

I have always been fascinated by and even envied reporters, editors and news people for their efforts in getting the needed news out to the people.

I would at times try my hand at putting down something that was bothering me or that I had learned. I would read it later, hear how silly it sounded, and then throw it away.

Recently I got up enough courage to send something in. Knowing that our young editor had been raised properly and taught to respect his elders I felt that he wouldn't just tell me that he couldn't print such junk and would submit it for print if he didn't consider it too controversial. And that is what he did.

Now I am a journalist – a writer of words that other people read. Oh what a great guy I am!

I try a couple of more pieces. I get them printed. Now I can go to the post office, the favorite coffee spots, the grocery store and I can imagine that people are thinking "here he comes again, that wonderful writer".

But of late when I give my big "hello George" or "hello Jack" they don't look at me or they will mumble something or become distracted just before I get to them.

I am slow, that I will admit. I have never split an atom with my brain power. I finally realized my friends don't want to be friends if I write. I might blaze something across the headline that has their name on it.

So it came to me – FOOL, this is it, your glory days are over. I cannot afford to alienate my friends and embarrass my family for such foolishness. I have been warned about that. THEY might get me someday (I have been threatened with THEY all my life and I still don't know who THEY are).

But I will throw in the towel. I will get myself a pair of those little hush-puppy shoes that old men wear. I will let my shoulders and neck sink down into a pair of those purple or dull orange colored jump suits that old men wear where the back pockets slap together as they slide along. I will go around muttering incoherent statements that no one cares to hear and spend my time getting in women-folks' way.

Yes, this is it for me. I am hanging up my spurs. Even Superman fell off his horse recently and as Chief Joseph said, "I will fight no more forever".

Today I found myself parking in the filled lot at Wal-Mart. Since I am through with thinking it took me a while to remember why I was there. I got out anyway, a whipped shell of a man. Now I was raised to believe that if you told a lie that you could be struck in tender places by lightning. I was in the army before I saw and heard people lie without getting zapped. I still give it serious thought before telling one.

What I am about to say really happened. Ahead of me walked a woman with articles under both arms. Something fell out of her arms without her detecting it. A teenager came from between the cars and scooped it up. In his haste he came face to face with me. He was going in the opposite direction of the lady who had dropped it. I stuck out my hand and said that I was going inside and that I would give it to her.

I went inside, looked around, and there she was in the returns line. She said "Oh thank you! I was going to return this and I thought I had left it at home".

It felt good. I felt alive again. I stood straighter, I bent over and stuck one trouser leg in my boot (any cowboy can understand how good that feels).

No, I am not buying those hush-puppy shoes. It came to me that my real friends would not leave me. Anything that I do is usually OK with them. They have ruled out me flapping my arms and running down the street in front of the library. They feel that such behavior would be more than they could back me on.

I hate injustice to my fellow man, I deplore dishonesty.

Being in the retail business in this county for 17 years I can tell you that 80 percent of our people are good, honest, decent, and kind folks. 20 percent are bad. I think that 20 percent are the THEY that I have been threatened with all my life.

You 20 percent better watch out because I am out there watching you and I am a REPORTER now.

To our young newspaper editor: If THEY ever bother you for voicing your opinion, do not give up hope. Before you strap your possessions to your vehicles like my mother's people leaving Oklahoma in the dust bowl days, you let me know. I know a lot of that 80 percent around here. If we can't change your mind, at least we can see that you get to go in an air-conditioned UHAUL and get to stay and dine in the best accommodations along the way.

42. THE GOOD SAMARITAN

In the last few years, I have had the habit (some say a bad habit) of taking my little Jeep and seeking out an off-the-road trail or logging trail, old home site, abandoned cemetery, etc.

Last summer I had taken one of these adventures and had gone further back into no-no land than I had thought, and spent considerable time checking out an old forgotten historical spot that I had been looking for. Late afternoon had approached. Returning to the jeep, I turned the key and it would not start. I know to keep gasoline. I know to keep air in the tires and to have a strong battery; the rest is left to the specialists.

Knowing where the main farm-to-market road is, I start walking. After reaching it, I still felt like I was nowhere, and saw no signs of human life.

Sometime later, I heard a rumbling sound some distance behind me. This is it, help is coming, I thought. So as not to appear anxious, I waited until the sound was near before I turned. There was a big, beautifully shiny pickup truck and the noise came from its boom-box music system. As he passed, I recognized a young white man that I had seen at intersections numerous times, shaking his head in time with his "music?" Well, he just shook and "boom-boomed" right on by. I felt my first panic, feeling like I wasn't even there.

Later there was another sound behind me, and I just knew this was it. This time I was not as calm. I stopped, turned and started waving my arms. Coming was an older model car containing an elderly white man that I had also seen in town and had often wondered if he should be allowed to drive the streets. When he saw me, he leaned over, locked the passenger side door and increased his speed a little, holding the wheel like he was on the Indianapolis Speedway.

My new hopes were gone, so I trudged on. I had passed a rutted road leading into the woods. Soon, I heard the obvious sounds of an old engine laboring under the strain of a load, probably of timber. Without turning, I heard it turn onto the path that I had crossed. Then I heard it stop. Soon it came up behind me, a black man in his late 30s behind the wheel with a load of pulpwood on his truck.

"You need help?" he asked.

"Well my Jeep won't start back down the road", I said. "Get in and we will go look at it", he replied. Laboring, we made our way back. He looked under the hood, tried to start it – nothing. "Well, I have some tools at home, let's pull it there and see what we find", he said. We used a pull chain, and I steered behind looking at the pulpwood for guidance. We turned down the little trail, went a good ways, and stopped. We were at a small cabin in the woods.

He came back and we unhooked, he went into the house, returned with two cans of cold Coke, one for him and one for me. He went to a shed and returned with a handful of tools. He raised the Jeep's hood and started unscrewing things. Soon he said "Try it now."

I did, it started. He said, "A coil wire had jumped off." I said, "How can I repay you?" He said to come on in the house and meet his family. It was a family consisting of a beautiful wife and three well-mannered pre-teen children. The wife asked me to stay and eat. I told her I would love to (the absolute truth), but that I had better let someone know where I was.

Now, who do you think that I will wish gets all the good things in life? Do you think it will be the young white man that seems to care for no one or anything but his boom-boom? Or will it be the old white man that seems to be afraid to get involved? Or would it be the young black man that I would stand back-to-back with and help defend him against his opponents?

And who do you think got a Christmas card from me, hoping that all was well and saying to let me know if I can help in any way?

Cletus Harvey on Booger

43. LESSONS FROM A HORSE

It was nearing the time for my eighth birthday. I always stood in the door opening of the school bus, and when the driver pulled the lever I jumped and hit the ground running up the dirt road to the house and barns.

Near the barn, I would see the old pickup and trailer that the Brogdon Ranch cowboys used. Nearing the trailer, I could see that one slat of the trailer door was lying on the ground.

Cigarette smoke was coming from both sides of the pickup, so I knew that the cowboys were inside. Looking through the side boards, I saw the ugliest creature that I had ever seen. Staring at me was what appeared to be a horse.

It had small, beady eyes that were set off-center, little ears that were laid back, and it was quite obvious that he didn't like me or probably anything else.

Seeing me in their rearview mirror, the cowboys got out and, without a word, they began trying to unload it. It twisted; it jumped; it kicked. Finally getting it tied to the lot fence, one cowboy said "Enjoy. But watch him, he's a booger" and they drove away. And there stood my birthday present.

For the next two years I learned very little at school. I knew the teachers were talking but my mind was on how I might get one up on that tornado named Booger.

If he was in the pasture, there was no catching him, until he got hungry enough for hay. Then you could run and slam the gate shut. My saddle was soon in tatters where I would have to bail off when he would run under something.

Sometimes he would run to me and act as if he was going to put his head in the bridle and then in a flash he would be gone. Other times, he would put his head in it and stand like a little angel while I saddled him – but the second I was in the saddle, the battle was on.

Once when I was letting him drink from a stock pond, I took my feet from the stirrups and relaxed a little. With his head down, he still dumped me in the water.

A city cousin was visiting and wanted to ride behind me. Booger broke into a run and headed straight for my mother's low clothes lines. It was November and the geese and ducks were traveling. I said "duck" and my cousin said "where?" and I looked back to see him do a cartwheel.

The end came when it took four good horses and four good cowboys to get a rope on him, after he had run through a farmer's cornfield causing considerable damage.

My dad said enough was enough and that I was not going to have sense enough to pull a boot on my right foot if I didn't start learning in school – and that he wanted that thing off the place.

So the Brogdon Ranch boys carried old Booger off to the local sale barn. Peeking through the slats at him, he did not look alarmed. He looked as if he was glad to be off on a new adventure.

For a while after that, if I saw a boy somewhere that looked happy but also showed signs that he couldn't work the ABC's or two plus two, I would ask him if he owned a horse.

44. ALARM SYSTEM A NICE SLEEP AID

There is nothing better than the feeling of having a peaceful sleep at home feeling safe and secure.

There is still, and probably always will be, a certain amount of the population that would rather steal something than to get an honest job. They can set their own hours that way.

Twice in the last two months, our great home alarm system, furnished by G&G Lock Co., has been set off by someone trying to enter an outside building after midnight. Within two minutes of the alarm going off, the night dispatcher at G&G will call you, you give them your code name, and they ask if you want police service. If you say yes, within 10 minutes at least two of our wonderful police officers will respond. Thieves can forget it – "it ain't going to happen, Hoss", as a dear friend, now deceased, used to tell me. They are just on their way to free room and board at our local jail.

Buying an alarm is the best money that can be spent if you value your possessions and property.

45. YOUTH IS A STATE OF MIND

Age and aging may very well be a mind set. Through the years, I have known people who seemed old at 18 and those who seemed young at 80.

My early years, from about 6 until 15, were spent in a North Texas farming community. My father pumped a small oil lease surrounded by farms. My schoolmates had to work farms, but I was a free spirit and roamed the country on horseback.

My classmates' parents called me "Billy the Kid" and said I wouldn't live to be 21. (I made that milestone.)

We moved from there to a rough and rowdy oil field town. I know now that I took some unnecessary chances, but survived. The Army called, and the townspeople said that (because of the chances that I took) I would never come home. (I did.)

During my years in the oil industry, I would volunteer for the hard and dangerous things, and people said "He is going to get his (any day now)."

I made it through that.

Then fate brought me to the beautiful town of Nacogdoches.

I bought and operated a business that catered to young people. My mental and physical being was reset by about 20 years.

I was interested in their lives, and I want to feel that they listened when I gave advice.

They are still out there, in our fire and police departments (don't call them cops; they deserve the respect to be called police), in our hospitals, in our city and county government. When they fail at something, they pick themselves up and try again.

I show respect and compassion to old people and will even listen to their same stories over and over, but when you say, "What a beautiful day" and they say "We could use some rain", I'm out of there.

With some people, the glass is always half empty, instead of half full.

We young folks just greet the day with optimism and hope, and when we fail we just get up and try again.

46. DEFENDING HIS FRIENDS

There are few (if any) people living in Nacogdoches today who have given more of themselves to improve the downtown than Dr. R. W. Gruebel and Jo Ellen Carlson.

Much of their waking hours are spent at hard labor, restoring and beautifying our downtown buildings and homes. They give time to committees and attend town meetings, discussing the things that will benefit those of us who live here. Their honesty, compassion and integrity are above any question. This brings us to the reason for my writing.

They have been criticized for wanting to have the control over their own property.

The complainers hide behind the media and don't have the nerve to reveal their names and to confront them face to face.

Everyone who knows me also knows that an attack on any friend of mine will not go unchallenged.

I have plenty of time on hand and a lot of my friends work and don't have the time to defend themselves. So, if you feel that you have need to bad mouth a friend of mine, contact me, and we will meet in private and on private property and we will discuss the issue one on one.

47. WE GOOF AGAIN

We as citizens have given away another one of our constitutional rights.

Our elected officials in the great state of Texas have just recently granted us permission (with rules, regulations, and fees attached) to do just what our constitution has always said that we could do – carry firearms. Now, if we will pay a fee, take firearms training and pass a morals test, we can carry a firearm. Isn't that wonderful?

You obtain a legal permit, then try walking into a grocery, or any other place that sells intoxicating beverages, show a pistol bulging out of your shirt, and just see how fast you end up in the cross-bar hotel with your hands cuffed behind your back, trying to get your legal permit out of your pocket with your teeth and crying that there must be some mistake.

And now, when you load your family up for a visit to Aunt Sally's in Houston (first mistake), and the police pull you over for driving too slow, they find your old varmint pistol under the seat and you have no permit.

I fear that you will have to sell the car and borrow money for a lawyer to defend yourself concerning a right you already had. But if the law stops an undetected killer, doper or rapist because he has a taillight out, and he is surrounded by guns but has a legal permit, they will just tell him to get the light fixed and wish him a good day.

I ran a business and often had large sums of cash on me. I worked for an oil company where my job took me into territory where angels feared to tread. I carried a gun.

No, I will not seek a permit.

No, I will not pay for firearm instructions – because the U.S. Army has already spent thousands on me.

No, I will not submit to a morals test where the tester may not have as many good ones as I have.

No, I will not pay the fee for a permit that will enable my name to be hooked into some government computer as a possible gun-toting maniac.

If a crazed fiend is intent upon your demise, it will matter not if you have a gun in each hand and a hand grenade in your mouth. He can still find a way to get to you. But most criminals are cowards, concerned only with dominating you and your possessions. I believe in negotiations and the surprise appearance of a gun upon any scene will cause negotiations to begin.

I have a great respect for law enforcement and I will never try to hide a weapon from them. They are all overworked and underpaid. We all have to take some of the responsibility for our own protection.

We are all fortunate to have in our county one of the most truly honorable district judges in Texas; and as the old saying goes, I had rather take my chances facing him and twelve of my neighbors for my actions than to face six pallbearers.

48. ON THE TRAFFIC LIGHTS

At the time of this writing, it is 3 p.m., Friday, July 18. I have just completed a fact-finding drive of some of our city's most dangerous streets, for the purpose of seeing first-hand the actions of the existing traffic lights. With the following, I will try to explain the purpose and the results.

We have had a rash of accidents, and even deaths, at some of these locations: 1) University and East Austin; 2) University and the north loop; but, most importantly, 3) Appleby Sand and the loop, at the high school.

Newspaper reports, law enforcement reports and TV reports seem to rush to judgment as to who is to blame. We say "Well, such things are handled in a court of law." But that's not so. Human nature being as it is, if a person that has been killed is accused by suggestion, rumor, eye witness or any other means, he cannot defend himself, and 90 percent will always blame them, regardless of the court's decision. Their family and friends will forever have this stigma to mar their wonderful memories.

Now, here are the findings of my little check on these traffic lights. We now have a new system that, in my opinion, simply invites tragedy. There are few – if any – amber lights. Lights rapidly switch from green to red and red to green. At any speed, you have to gamble with your life and the lives of others because you could not possible react quickly enough as the light changes from green to red. Also, there is a new red arrow for turns. All my driving life, an arrow meant turn now. While watching frantically in six directions and an arrow – of any color – shows my turn, my reflexes react and I might attempt it.

I feel sure that lights are controlled by computers, and I know that it will take a computer expert a very short time to change the lights, should this letter be printed. So, I ask the readers to go out shortly after reading this to see for yourself what is happening. It may be one of your loved ones accused of causing a horrible accident tomorrow.

49. OBNOXIOUS STICKERS

Upon our streets there is a well-used Chrysler New Yorker. Prominently displayed on it is a sticker that reads: "If you don't like the way I drive, call 1-800-EAT S---".

This car has an expired license. Only a rear license is displayed, and it is nearly unreadable. State law required both rear and front license plates displayed.

Another car in town is in such bad shape that if a dealer should let it pass inspection, their license for doing state inspections should be revoked. It displays a sticker that reads: "This is not the Mayflower, but your daughter came across in the back seat!"

No, no, no – until just a few short years ago this was the "old Texas". It took a pure fool to insult a Texan. There were people that met their maker for saying the wrong word or for kicking a man's dog.

These signs thrown in people's faces are much more offensive than a flag that depicts a culture that fought and died for something they believed in. This is not a racial thing. One vehicle is driven by the black race; the other by whites. This is human low-life trying to force their perverse filth down the throats of decent people. They feel that the fear of law suits, physical harm, getting involved, sneaky retaliation against the complainant or his family, will cause people to just take the insults and go on.

But watch it out there, I know who you are, and there are still a few "old Texans" out there that will still defend themselves, friends, and neighbors against insults, although age may overtake me someday (not yet) and render me helpless to fight back. Until that time, don't take the chance of placing an insult in my view. If you do, it would be easier for you to place the stickers on your bumper than the window, because paper and glass are easier to digest than a chrome bumper.

50. NOTHING TO DEBATE ON TORTURE

Being raised a Texan and an American provided a wonderful world for me.

First, as a Texan, people from other states respected you, and as an American, you had the respect of other countries.

Along with these honors, you had responsibility. I allowed no abuse or mistreatment of any living thing – people, animal or creature. I would act quickly to help. I have even walked around ants, if they were in their own territory. Living in rattlesnake country, they were left alone to go on their way if they posed no threat.

I once administered quick justice to a fellow student who had shoved a wheelchair patient down a hall at a rapid pace and then laughed.

Entering the Army, other soldiers would say "Don't mess with Tex". And I know that when in a foreign country, I would be protected by the "Geneva Conventions".

Now, to my point: We have come to the point in time where our elected officials "elected to help and protect us" are debating water boarding and torture.

The only torture that 80 percent of these officials have had may have been: 1) Time out at home, 2) No television, 3) No computer games, 4) No automobile to drive to high school, and 5) Not getting to join a fraternity or sorority in college.

Here is how they could learn firsthand about "water boarding".

A person very close to me just had a heart pacemaker installed. You are placed on a hard bench about 2 feet wide. Your arms and legs are strapped tight. Your body is covered with thick insulated material. Your face is covered with a hood. Then you are asked if you are alright. "Oh, yes; I am wonderful and having a great time." And I guarantee you that if they asked "Now, we believe that the world is flat; what do you believe?" your answer would be "Yes, definitely, it is flat, and I have walked to the edge and looked over."

We will always have good people and bad people. But let's keep them separated by law and regain our place in the world as the country that rides in wearing the white hats. Instead of like other countries who hear "Get out of our country", they will say "Thank the Lord for the United States of America".

51. MOURNING A CLOSING

The ladies of Nacogdoches have lost again.

John Schmidt and Phyllis Anderson worked hard to offer them a chance to put a little more sunshine (one can't ever have enough) into their everyday lives. A chance for grandmothers to show their daughters and granddaughters that life can exist past fast foods, past placing your order with the clown and riding down the road eating and drinking from plastic and Styrofoam. A world that could offer them real china cups and plates and linen tablecloths spread over beautiful antique tables. Women's organizations and clubs or just a few friends could give advance notice and be treated royally.

Still, many chose to hold their gatherings in some room covered with fold-out tables, equipped with trays to carry through a buffet line and get all you want of something. Doesn't matter what, just something.

Well, Schmidt's has sold (why is their business) and an outsider has bought (why is their business), and your chances of going there are over and gone.

I still tell you what the ladies of tiny Jefferson, Texas (who have not obeyed or listened to a man in 30 years) would have done.

They would have organized and gone to the new owner and said, "What can we do to keep this going? We will lead a fund drive, we will volunteer help. This place is your gold mine compared to placing a few shoes and dress racks in the space."

Many people, even some in my own family, feel everything has to be done to make a money profit.

Phyllis Anderson was not doing this for monetary gain. She is quite secure in assets. She likes people and she likes to be involved in something that makes a difference in people's lives.

She is talented and versatile, and she will bounce back and go on to other things. Schmidt will get to enjoy a long-earned leisure.

We, in Nacogdoches, are the losers.

52. FIXING THE SOGGY NEWSPAPER

I recently complained about a soggy Sunday newspaper. I want to thank "The Daily Sentinel" and its circulation department for the prompt attention and dedication to good service.

My Sunday papers have since been double-wrapped and tied tight. My daily papers have all been tied up.

It was not the threat of attorneys that caused this. This scares no one these days. It was their desire to do a good job. Now if our young editor could work with the Legislature to get us two relaxing Sundays in each week, all would be well.

Editor's note: We're afraid our influence in the Legislature isn't that great these days.

53. THANK YOU TO CLETUS HARVEY

Thank you, Cletus Harvey, for the nice letter today. You are a nice man.

For all you folks who don't like for me to use Sgt. B. York, get used to it. I don't change. How many Sgt. Yorks do you know in Nacogdoches?

Yes, Cletus, I have read all of your letters, and enjoy them. Yes, I have made it on my own – wasn't easy. I have been around some good folks.

Yes, I did fight for this country. And I came back with two bronze stars. I love this country.

If I ever got a handout, I don't know what year it was. I sure hope the readers know what moxie is. I also donate money to many. I get about three to five letters a week asking for money. I even got one from Toys for Tots. I had a stick horse when I grew up in New Camp, Chireno. And I did not, will not ever, miss Korea.

I was a soldier, I am a soldier, I will always be a soldier.

Sgt. Bobby York

Nacogdoches

Response from Cletus Harvey:

The Sgt. York of WWI fame would be proud that our Sgt. York is carrying on his name.

Richard Johnson

54. A TRIBUTE TO THE MAYOR

Some years back there was a song that went something like this: "I grew up on Wayside Drive. Had to fight just to stay alive."

Some years back "trying to escape this kind of environment" a young man rode into the small town of Nacogdoches "possibly on a load of watermelon". He couldn't spell the word, but he hoped that this would be a spot where he could plant roots, prosper and carve himself out an honorable, peaceful place in life. His only visible assets were bright blue eyes, broad shoulders, strong arms and hands. He liked all people and, like Will Rogers, he never met a man he didn't like, and wished to be in public service. The local police chief recognized his potential and hired him. He learned the law quickly and soon became the one the chief greatly depended on.

He showed no favoritism when it came to the law; he was fair, personable and kind. One person told me that it was a pleasure to have him arrest you because he was so nice to you.

But like many small towns, there are a certain few who fear to release any power and control. The workings of the police force became so political and unorganized that he thought of finding a business to go into.

He did not fear hard work, and he knew how to use a hammer and saw as well as how to patch and repair almost anything. So he set out to carve his niche in life. I stood inside a downtown building for five years surrounded by glass that allowed me to witness the activities of the square. Business operators would start arriving from 8 a.m. to 10 a.m. This man would usually be there to visit with them a few minutes and, with his winning personality, make their coming day look brighter.

I have watched him listen just as intently to the newest derelict on the street as he did a bank president. There is no such thing as "the little people" in his mind. Everyone is a person.

He likes all people, and he loves Nacogdoches, and it has recently paid off for him.

His name is Richard Johnson, and he is the major of Nacogdoches.

55. UNSUNG HEROES

A view of the world through the window of a hospital room is much different than having early morning coffee at the office or driving through the fast food outlet and getting a biscuit on the run.

Things move at a slower pace. You watch the people arrive to start their day. Some doctors are leaving after performing surgery on one patient, then rushing to their office to see what they can do to help someone else.

Veteran nurses arrive to relive others who have completed a 12-hour shift and may have to return in eight hours. Seasoned aides go through their day quietly monitoring and recording the vitals of their patients. Young eager assistants hold down two jobs and train hard to become what they have dreamed of becoming – a nurse. Dietary personnel help distribute three meals a day that require much preparation for the individual needs of each patient. Custodians have to clean the vast amount of debris that results from hour-to-hour needs of the patients. Maintenance people constantly try to keep equipment and machinery fine-tuned. Office people struggle constantly to stay up with the constant change of government regulations. Administration tries to stay on top of a unit that is much more complicated than any city government. Therapists try to get people back on their feet while meeting resistance from some who would rather just quit and give up. Throughout the day and night, there is need for the help of firemen, police, emergency personnel and volunteers, such as the wonderful pink ladies who give of themselves to help those in need.

These people are not working for the money alone. They are dedicated, concerned, helpful, caring people who believe in what they do.

And, in doing so, they are often taken advantage of, disrespected, and much ignored by the people who need them the most.

I feel that a big part of a security guard's job should be to listen and watch for any sign of disrespect or abuse of any hospital employee and to act swiftly in their defense.

Nacogdoches Medical Center

Cletus Harvey and Rom Holmes

56. IN LOVING REMEMBRANCE OF ROM HOLMES

A tall rugged man rode into town
Got off his horse and looked around.
He said to his partner "Well I guess
We need to get tough, let's clean up this mess."
Crime was everywhere in the streets of the town.
When they finished their job no one could be found.
A man with this character all so full of pride
Will make any "evil thing" get up and ride.
It's not just a person standing on a floor;
It's everything that makes a man what he stands for.
His pride, his character, his morals, his strength
Are things we all reach for, even at great lengths.
To cherish this man let's capture him on film
Because when I grow up I want to be just like HIM!

To the last of the BEST.
This is for you.
Your Friend,
David Perkins

PawPaw - running with good company

57. WORDS TO LIVE BY

To Ryan Christopher Bruning from his PawPaw

When you were brought to the lobby 10 years ago for us to see, I knew that you were special by the way you were taking in all that you could see of this new world.

In this 10 years, you have excelled in your endeavors, sports, school, you are kind and caring toward your little brother and sister, polite and respectful. You are everything that your PawPaw could have wanted in a grandson.

In your 10 years you have already seen more changes and events happen in the world than I could have imagined, even in my Buck Rogers days.

My time went from seeing people ride their horses into town, to a passenger plane launched the size of a football field.

The rapid change in morals, standards, attitudes and conduct scare your PawPaw (yes, I can have fear, too). I find myself withdrawing from association when possible.

At your age, I had my own front-row seat in the movie theater. My conduct was shaped by the likes of Gene Autry, Buck Jones, and the Lone Ranger.

Following are some of the things that PawPaw would like for you to mold into your life and then go forward and live life to the fullest.

Your PawPaw cannot abide by rude behavior.

1. Be kind and protective to children and animals.
2. No one can win all the time, so when you are knocked down, pick yourself up, dust yourself off, and get back in the game.
3. Do not tamper with anyone's pride, dignity or self-respect, regardless of race, creed, color or position in life.
4. When you hear foul language used in any situation, put a stop to it immediately.
5. When you witness abuse or mistreatment of any living thing, act immediately, and if you feel the situation is more than you can handle alone, call for backup. We have the bravest, most qualified law personnel in the world.

I hope to have time left to tell you all that Gene, Buck, and the Lone Ranger taught me.

You are a wonderful grandson, and PawPaw loves you very much.

58. A POSSIBLE SOLUTION TO THE PROBLEMS WITH THE U.S. POSTAL SERVICE

The delivery of the mail was one of the biggest stabilizers of early America.

The Pony Express riders and stage coach drivers had to be brave, in excellent physical condition and honest above approach. They had to face wild Indians, wild animals, bandits, robbers and vicious weather. But the mail had to go through.

Growing up on the high plains of Texas, where neighbors were at least a mile apart, the mail was their window to the world.

Mailmen, as they were called then, were respected by all and became like members of the families. If one became stranded by weather or breakdown, the word traveled, and they were rescued by horse or tractor or automobile, and their route was completed.

Today's postal persons hold basically to the same standards. They are courteous, physically fit, helpful and our watchdogs for crime in our neighborhoods, and will push themselves to great lengths to see that the mail goes through.

Cut the United States mail? No. Let's trim the excessive salaries from the top. Double the employees' salaries and produce all mail boxes with the United States seal on them, and then let the company be owned by the workers' pension fund.

59. DREAM COMES TRUE

"Even though we face the difficulties of today and tomorrow, I still have a dream… I have a dream that one day on the red hills of Georgia the sons of former slaves and the sons of former slave owners will be able to sit down together at the table of brotherhood."

Martin Luther King Jr., Aug. 28, 1963

60. MASTER STORYTELLER SPINS TALES FROM THE GRAVES IN THE OLDEST TOWN IN TEXAS
Article by Jill Kerr

One of the most popular events at the Nine Flags Festival according to event coordinator Diana Walker will be when Cletus Harvey tells his tales from the oldest cemetery in Texas. Promising to add some post-Halloween thrills and chills to this historic Christmas celebration, Harvey, who has been giving tours of the Oak Grove Cemetery since 1986, will lead groups through this history-rich area of Nacogdoches during the festival weekend.

Nacogdoches has the distinct honor of hosting this folklorist and storyteller for the Festival. Mr. Harvey started by giving tours to sixth graders. Teaching the children to respect the graves and history the cemetery holds. He is now sharing his knowledge with all those interested in hearing the stories of Texas' past, and his participation in the event promises to add an entertaining glimpse into Nacogdoches' rich history.

Mr. Harvey owned a western wear store for seventeen years and this business has helped develop his interest in history. Through his store Mr. Harvey has made the acquaintance of many locals who have provided him with colorful stories of Nacogdoches County. These personal stories give a unique look at history. Stories of murder, love, gain and loss are the tales that are used to make the cemetery come alive. The cemetery contains such notable historic figures as Thomas J. Rusk, Texas' first Senator, and the tragic story of his death. Mr. Harvey believes the cemetery is a valuable resource, and the stories he shares give a glimpse of the interesting history of Nacogdoches.

This event is a great way to combine the entertainment of good storytelling with the education of Nacogdoches' rich history. Mr. Harvey's stories are sure to add a dose of excitement and interest to the already full slate of entertaining activities planned for the Festival. Festival-goers can enjoy Harvey's historical tales from 10:00am to 3:00pm at the Oak Grove Cemetery on Saturday, December 5th. For more information concerning this event or any of the Nine Flags Festival events, call toll free 1-888-564-7351.

61. RECALLING ANNE MILLARD

I was out of town somewhere when Anne Millard made her exit from life's stage and, except for the shock and grief, it was all over by the time I learned of it.

When I left town, she was so active. She seemed to be everywhere at once. She was a spark and ignition with the efforts to revitalize downtown. She was on committees, planned activities, and organized events.

Shortly before I left, she had told me that she was planning a documentary film on early Nacogdoches. Since she knew all about my studies on Sam Houston, she honored me by asking me to play the part. She also asked me who I thought was the biggest hero in the Revolution. I told her my pick would be James Bonham, because he had two chances to stay out of the Alamo, where he faced certain death, but his pride and loyalty made him ride back in.

She also said she intended to have a part for her son, George Millard III. The planned documentary never happened, and when her torch fell, someone else picked it up and ran on. That's the way of life.

Last Saturday, the paper showed a front-page picture of a young man holding five beautiful strawberries in his hand. The article stated that he had raised 92,000 plants and gave his location.

I left immediately for that location.

When I slipped from my car, he was already walking toward me with hand outstretched.

These were his first words, "Do you think my mother would be proud of me?" I think my answer was "She was always proud of you."

But that wasn't enough. So George Millard III, here is my answer to you.

I deeply believe that she is with you when you are working hard to raise the best strawberries possible. She is with you when you happily give your time and tractor and hay wagon, which you yourself drive, to allow free rides during the Christmas festival. She is there when you help display the silver angel that was purchased in her honor, which is displayed on the downtown square during Christmas holidays.

Yes, she was and is proud of you, George Millard III. And I am proud of you. And others who are fortunate enough to be greeted with a handshake and a look into your sincere, trustful face are proud that they got to meet you.

And I know who was going to play the loyal Bonham.

62. CRACKING UP IN HOUSTON

I am an adult male who has had his share of nearly fatal escapes and experiences. I have even dangled at the end of my safety belt for nearly an hour waiting for rescue after my feet slipped walking derricks one cold, icy night in West Texas. I have nerves of steel.

But there is one place that can make me crack and lose it all: Houston.

My little Jeep and I are aging together. Its advanced mileage and worn parts do just fine under civilized circumstances and when it is handled gently. Everything goes just right until you pass Livingston; but as you approach Splendora and past, things seem to change. You grip the wheel a little tighter, you step up the speed some. By the time you reach Kingwood and are headed to Humble, your mouth is dry, eyes are slightly bugged, and you are fully alert.

From Humble on, it is pure Panicsville. You try to hide the fact that you are from Hicksville, but you cannot. They curse you, they wave fists at you, and they spit, frown, growl, and threaten your family as they speed by you at an ungodly pace.

Some have told me horror stories of having guns pointed at them.

When you finally dare try an exit and get your newly rock-chipped, poor little Jeep out of the madness, you know you need gas and a rest room. You are not allowed the rest room until you get gas. Gas pump says "insert card". I use cash; I have no card. Pump says "lift nozzle"; I do. It says "push button for cash", it says "pay at office before pumping gas". I look around and find that I am being looked at through a hole in the glass by a person in desert clothing. No gun is visible, but you feel its presence. You lay $10 on the counter and say "give me $10 worth". "OK" he says. Then lift nozzle, push button for cash, replace nozzle. I am not going to do it; I want what I had paid for. I return to the booth. I tell him that there is still no gas. "OK" he says and I return to the nozzle. Nothing yet. I look up to see an "I'm in charge grin" inside the booth. Now here is the scary part. Here is where proponents of the right to be armed may have a point.

I consider myself a rational person. But my nerves had been drawn thin; my money was not getting what had been paid for. I knew he was armed, maybe even had it in his hand. My gun was in the Jeep within reach. But before I could make a rational, or a very foolish, decision, the pump started and I came back to semi-reality.

My purpose in Houston was accomplished and I was able to get out of it with some degree of sanity.

After careful consideration I have decided what can be done with Houston.

A number of us have loved ones there. There are a number of good people in the city.

Here is what can be done. The TEC can devise a test that will without a doubt determine whether you are a good person or bad.

We can get the Democratic Party to set up an agency that will make the good people relocate, give them assistance with this relocating, and supply jobs wherever they go.

The bad would have to stay in Houston and could not leave. Not only that, we would need few jails because the county sheriffs in Texas could run a bus shuttle into Houston and dump our bad on them. They should not be allowed to entice our good people into Houston by rodeos or ballgames or fairs, where they could be mugged, robbed, or killed.

They could do all of these things to each other and have a ball.

But you say they have good hospitals there. Fine, let helicopters lift the doctors and nurses and aides into every shift. Also the patients in and out.

There has to be a good side to Houston and that's the best that I can do.

63. ON THE BAREFOOT GIRL

In the letter column (Aug. 23) Mrs. McCullough was horrified that the photo run in our paper of the recent graduation at SFA was of a young girl crossing the stage barefooted and raising her gown to her thighs.

Mrs. McCullough has every reason and right to be outraged. So should the students and parents of the other 799 people that crossed the stage to receive diplomas. A degree earned after all the sacrifices, dedication and hard work should be treated with dignity and respect by all involved.

But where should the blame be placed? It should fall on the shoulders of the policy makers of SFA. Anyone who paid their money, and respects the guidelines and rules laid down, should be able to trust their superiors and administrators to see that no person crossing that stage did anything that distracted from their chance to have their day of full glory.

We citizens would not have known about these things if we were not shown in the news.

I have friends that feel that it is favorable to refer to our paper as the "Daily Senile" or the "Daily Silly". I just smile to myself and remember that they were not here 20 years ago when the newspaper was often afraid to print something for the many to see because it might offend the handful in control.

64. BOOMTOWN MEMORIES

I was about 6 years old when my parents left the beautiful ranch land of the Texas Panhandle and moved into the hustle and bustle of a small Texas oil boomtown.

Living quarters were scarce – no homes for sale or lease. Some lived in tents.

We found a duplex to rent near downtown. Each side had a front door and a back door, and they shared a porch on each end.

A family with the name Bynum lived in the other duplex. They had a son my age named Carl.

I remember that I tolerated Carl, but for some reason we were never that close.

Our location allowed us to hear the rough and rowdy sounds of downtown to the east and the music and sounds of the largest and loudest water hole, a beer joint named "The Owl's Inn" that was in that part of Texas.

It was on a Saturday, probably between noon and 1 p.m. that Carl ran through the front door and out the back where I was. He was excited, wild-eyed, and out of breath. When he had calmed some, he got the words out that Gene Autry was inside The Owl's Inn, and his Cadillac and horse trailer with his horse, Champion, was parked outside.

Little time was lost, and we ran the six blocks very quickly.

The road had deep ditches on each side, and we hid in the one close to the tavern, with just the tops of our heads and our eyes sticking up.

No one came out, and we waited and waited – probably two hours – and then it happened.

The door sprang open, and out came Gene with his big hat, his boots, and his pistols.

Every drunk, driller, roughneck, cowboy, and trucker in town was right behind him. He walked to the horse trailer, checked Champion, then to the door of his Cadillac, gracefully raised his hat to the drunks, and then he was gone.

Carl moved on to some other boomtown. We crossed paths four or five times in later years. We both were drafted in the Korean conflict, and I heard that he was killed on some ridge or hill, pork chop, pancake or something.

The times that we did talk we both concluded that Gene looked directly at us, and I know to this very day that Gene looked directly at me and tipped his hat to me and not to those drunks.

65. A GREAT ACCOMPLISHMENT

The Old Timers Breakfast has come and gone again, and appears to have been a success.

Mr. Abernethy was presented with the award honoring him for being the oldest man in attendance for what I believe was the seventh year. He stood graciously and respectfully answered a couple of questions and then sat down.

I am sure that he has many more accomplishments in his life, but there were none greater than the one I witnessed.

Most people had left the hotel to go on with their day, as we were leaving the parking lot. The south side parking was nearly empty as I pulled onto Hospital Street.

Dr. F. E. Abernethy, Mr. Abernethy's son and a person who has had many honors, titles and accomplishments rightfully bestowed upon him, had linked his right arm into his father's left arm and they were walking slowly across the lot.

They were talking, laughing and smiling as they walked, and for a few minutes there was no one else in this world but each other.

And I say that is the greatest accomplishment. To raise a son or daughter that honors, respects, cares, appreciates, and shows real concern for you.

66. CHIVALRY IS ALIVE AND WELL

Chivalry is still all around us. National news tells of racial conflict, color barriers, nationality discrimination, religious differences, and our young people going bad.

I have the opportunity of traveling much of our town daily and have always been a people watcher. So here are some of the things that I see daily.

As you get older, things seem to slow down. Walking becomes a little harder, and sight and balance can be a problem. In the past two weeks, I have seen two serious falls – one an elderly man, another a woman. Before I could get out of my car, people of all races and color were rushing to help. Little children will rush ahead to hold a door for someone having difficulty. More active women will give assistance to other women. Men will lock arms with another man in need.

Recent national tragedies have people from around the country trying to help. Our country is still intact and the greatest country in the world.

There will always be the bad, but our sheriff's officers and police officers are very qualified and will get them. The good people will always outnumber them.

67. NEIGHBOR'S PEACE AND QUIET IS BROKEN

I have lived on my street for 21 years. It is a pretty street, running from Appleby Sand Road (with a couple of sharp turns) to Logansport Road. For 19 years it was a quiet, rarely traveled street occupied by what I'll call mature people. We have had only one child raised on this street, a girl who grew into a beautiful red-haired lady and has gone forth out into the world.

So seldom were any of us in the street that we worried little when traffic and speed stated picking up, with people making short cuts to avoid many things (particularly the law) when they wished to speed. Now that we are getting some welcomed young folk with young children on our street, we don't need those fast driving fools around. Never have I seen one stopped but this is what I did see recently.

While performing the boring task of front yard grass mowing, I like to watch life in our neighborhood. An attractive lady that I recognize as a down-the-street neighbor had probably decided to run an errand. She suddenly stopped her car on the opposite side of my yard. Behind her was a police car containing two well-equipped officers. Lights were turning and flashing as bright as a New Orleans burlesque show. Both officers exited and approached each side of her car with caution. Now I have been around very few hardened criminals but this lady just didn't look the type. She just peered through the rear view mirror with alarm, hoping that they didn't demand that she get out and spread 'em, which would further embarrass her in her neighborhood.

The officer on the passenger side stood back a little, feet spread and ready to spring into action if need be. After taking some time to write a ticket (what horrible infraction could she have committed in such a short distance from home?) they released her, then followed her to the light at Appleby Sand just in case she tried to pull something else.

Isn't it a shame that two grown men couldn't find more to do than play a showdown at the O.K. Corral with a lady probably on her way to spend her money with our local merchants?

As this scene played out a dear friend had stopped to visit. As we stood in the driveway visiting, horrible noises started coming up Appleby Sand from the direction of Logansport Road. Sirens blared, horns honked, dogs barked, lights flashed. Oh it was serious business.

My friend, who spent many years in law enforcement and military investigation, now lives in the quiet town of Chireno. He said "My God, what do you think it is?" and then I said "My God, they are turning on our street" and then I said "My God they are stopping at my neighbor's house."

The fire engine slid to a stop. Two healthy young firemen leapt off and ran to the house. One began beating on the front door while one ran to the back. I feared that the excitement might get to my friend so I was thinking of getting him a chair when he said "Let's jump in my car and turn on the scanner to try and find out what's happening."

Just as two police cars roared up, the dispatcher was heard to say "No, it's 18xx Sandlewood or Saddlewood or Silkwood – not 18xx E. Austin."

Now how do you mistake that for something ending in E. Austin?

Teachers have told me for years that young people don't know how to follow instructions. This may have been a case in point.

The fire truck backed up into one of the few yards that actually have some children living there. The police cars pulled some maneuvers used in the Police Academy movies and they all sped away in a hubbub of horrible noises.

Just as they cleared the street we heard on the scanner that they could return to station, that the car fire on some Wood street was out. They didn't say whether it burned out or was put out. We don't feel that it rained anywhere in town that day so it was probably not put out by the rainwater.

There is a fine couple (past middle age) who are the owners of the house that was ambushed. The man of the house has had some slight health problems and we are all so fond of them that we self-appoint ourselves to keep an eye out for him when his wife has to be away. He loves to smoke a pipe (I smoked one for 19 years), but his wife doesn't like him to and neither do we because we all want him to stay with us for a good while.

Everything happened so suddenly that by the time my neighbor could get re-grouped from whatever it was he was doing, it was over.

My friend and I watched him come out to his driveway, look up and down the street, face headed into the sun, packing his pipe and trying to figure out what had happened.

Lo and behold here comes his wife driving in and finding him standing in the yard, smoking a pipe, with a bewildered look on his face.

My friend looked at me and in the silence I read his mind. It said that our beautiful street was just too nerve racking for him and he was headed back to the peace and quiet of Chireno.

Now I have my ace in the hole. If my neighbor cannot convince his wife that he heard fire trucks, police and noises at his doors and comes to me for help, I am going to tell him that if he mows my grass for two weeks I will tell his wife that indeed there were all of those on our street. If he doesn't agree I will say "No madam, I didn't see or hear a thing."

68. DEFENDING HOME HEALTH CARE

In a recent local police report, it was stated that a complainant had filed a report and that there had been numerous health-care people in and out.

Let's talk about that.

I have recently returned from a trip to the Texas Panhandle, where it had become my duty to supervise the care of a 96-year-old uncle. He had been a loving, caring uncle to me through the years and remained so until the end.

In his last few years of living alone and advancing age, his mind had been altered.

About six months ago I drove there (604 miles) and arranged for home health care for him. Three days after returning home, they contacted me to tell me they would not stay because he insisted on paying someone to carry him to the senior center to eat (an infraction of their rules).

When I returned, I was told that "those people" had stolen nearly everything in the house. A quick inventory showed that all valuables were intact, and most of the supposed missing items were found (none of them of any value).

I reinstated home health care and returned home. Two weeks later they informed me that they would stay no longer, but I could come and put him in a nursing home or, since his time was very limited, I might be able to get Hospice. I did (another 604 miles).

The home health organization is one of the most wonderful things that this country has set up. These people need to draw combat pay for what they do. The Hospice people are truly angels of mercy. They allow some people the chance to leave this world with dignity.

Before these people walk into a house to help, they should demand a full inventory be taken and should be allowed to supervise anyone coming or going. If there are any allegations of stealing going on, they should let the person stay alone unattended for about 12 hours. When they returned, the person would say "Wouldn't you like to have that pretty lamp over there? I will give it to you."

Susan Harvey Bruning, 1991

69. A LETTER TO HER GRANDPARENTS
By Susan Harvey Bruning

Dear Mama and Dada,

Just want you to know that I love you very much and am praying for you. Just like you said on the phone, Mama, operations like this are very common and successful. I'm sure y'all have heard the story of "Footprints in the Sand" and of how there are two sets of footprints as we walk through life, but in the hard times there are just one set, Christ's, for he is carrying us. Remember he is always with us and everything that happens is in his plan. I know he's going to be taking care of Dada. I love you both and will talk to y'all after the operation.

All My Love,
Suzi

BILLY BYRD

Football '45 '46; E Association '45 '46 '47; President of Senior Class '46 '47; Student Council '46 '47; Spanish Club '43 '44; Senior Spotlight; Who's Who in Physical Education '43 '44; Most Popular Boy '47.

70. MASTER SGT. BILLY BYRD

Billy Byrd and I started school together in a three-room building, with a storage shed for supplies and two out-houses – boys and girls, of course.

It was located on the high plains of Texas, a rocky hillside named Rocky Point.

We were both oil field brats, and bonded immediately. We defended each other from would-be trouble and stuck together as much as possible.

My family moved on to another field, and it was not until my freshman year that we moved back to the rowdy town where the high school was. Our friendship picked up where it had left off.

More than once through those years, if someone had a beef against me they had to confront Billy Byrd first.

He was honest (to a fault), loyal, strong, brave, kind to women, children and animals – and you might get a lecture if he saw you step on a bug.

But you knew that someone or something was in for trouble if those baby blue eyes flashed in anger.

Once, when one of those new drive-in movies was to open in a pasture near our hometown, I drove out to get Billy Byrd. His mother had already lectured him about places like that – that they had a possibility of being sinful.

So we told her that we were going into the town movie theater.

When we got about a mile away, he said "Stop this car".

I said "What's the matter?"

He said, "I can't lie to my mother."

We went back and told her the truth, and she said that she knew it all along but was glad that we came clean about it.

I was out of high school, knocking around from one job to another, more interested in improving my pool game than anything else. I was just what the Army was looking for, and they drafted me.

Billy Byrd stayed there, worked for a major oil company, and became master sergeant of our local National Guard.

Years went by without any contact, but I always knew that help was just a phone call away.

His wife said he ate his breakfast one morning, flashed that Billy Byrd smile, went out alone to work and was found about 10 a.m. dead of a heart attack.

Standing in a high plains cemetery, I had forgotten how hard a November wind could blow.

A little removed from the crowd of strangers (I probably knew some of them in the past, but no longer), I watched as the preacher's mouth moved but could not be heard because of the wind. I looked across the prairie and saw tumbleweed about four feet around suddenly break free of its roots. Rolling and bouncing along, it cleared a barbed wire fence and then was out of sight.

Roll on Master Sergeant Billy Byrd, and I will catch up with you some day.

71. EXCERPT FROM ARTICLE BY EMILY TARAVELLA

Cletus Harvey, a master storyteller in Nacogdoches, shared ghost stories with children Saturday night at "Scare on the Square".

I called him Monday to see how it went, and he said it was just as he'd hoped it would be.

"My aim was to explain to the children that we all hope we have a spirit within us that never dies, and it would stand to reason that after we're gone, that spirit stays around somewhere." He said "I wanted them to feel that if they have felt an unexplained presence around them, they should not fear it. That it would be a good spirit, because bad spirits would not be allowed the freedom to move around us."

At Halloween, there's a whole lot of talk about things that are scary and frightful.

But the idea of friendly spirits visiting some of their favorite places really isn't scary to me.

When it comes to ghosts and our favorite ghost stories, I think Mr. Harvey has the right idea.

(Emily Taravella is a staff writer for "The Daily Sentinel")

WOULD YOU LIKE
TO SEE
CLETUS HARVEY
BREAK HIS ▮▮ ??
Hmmmm?
WELL CHIP IN A BUCK
TO THE "CLETUS HARVEY
RODEO FUND". OLE' "CLETE"
WILL RIDE FOR THE #29
IN THE RODEO AT YAKIMA,
& THE PURSE WILL BE
SPLIT BETWEEN ALL
WHO CONTRIBUTE!
PAY NOW!

SUEDE BOOTS MARTHA!

Cletus Harv.
comin' out on
Mother-In-Law
Chute No. 5

72. A RODEO STAR?

Many, many years ago, I was stationed at the U. S. Army base at Fort Lewis, Washington. The Yakima Indian Reservation was nearby and they were to hold their annual rodeo.

Other soldiers were growing tired of my bragging about being a great rodeo star back in Texas.

So they made me put up or shut up. A pot was raised for entrance fees, posters placed around the base, bets made (probably more against me than for me) and I was entered in the bare-back ride. The big day came, and I had nothing to wear but Army fatigues and combat boots.

Any cowboy knows that without a real hat and real boots, despair would set in.

My time came, and as I started to climb the gate, a man standing by said "What size boot do you wear, cowboy?"

I answered "size 10". He sat down in the dirt, pulled off his boots and said "put these on".

He stood in the dirt until I made my ride. Then I thanked him, gave him his boots back, and shook his hand.

Now, those Indians against whom I was competing were wild and tough. It was quite obvious that they would attempt to rope and ride a tornado, if one was around. Even so, I placed third and strutted around for weeks until the first sergeant said he didn't want to hear any more about that (blank) rodeo.

Years went by, and one day I was un-boxing a shipment of Wrangler jeans in my store, and there on the pocket label of the trousers was the face of the man who had loaned me his boots – Mr. Jim Shoulders HIMSELF.

73. STIMULUS THAT WORKS

In another life, I had the good fortune to be employed by an oil and gas distributor in Houston that, among other businesses, owned one of the largest automobile sales and service agencies in Houston.

The owner began getting feedback from his employees and others that the average customer was not getting treated fairly at this agency, that the wealthy customer received most of their attention.

This man (who will remain unnamed) found a well-used station wagon, put on an old khaki shirt and a pair of overalls and scuffed up boots, and drove in.

Workers were running about; many passed by the man without looking his way. Finally, one said "Hey mister, move that thing over here out of the way." Other nice autos came in and received prompt attention.

Finally, one employee came by with the name "Manager" on his tag. The potential customer said, "Sir, could you help me?" The answer was "Be with you in a minute." The customer said, "No, I will speak to you right now. I am (name not revealed). Now, take me to the head office."

The man in charge recognized him immediately and asked, "What are you doing here?" Answer was, "I want every key to this place brought in and placed on this desk. Then I want you to fire every person here, except the janitors. They seem to be doing a good job."

"Then pack your things and get out."

This was done, and he and the janitors locked everything down. The agency was closed for one month.

During this time, it was completely re-staffed (except for the janitors) and as far as I know it is still one of the best operated agencies in the town of Houston.

74. EFFICIENT COURT SYSTEM

I was both honored and humbled last week. Honored that our court system would consider me qualified to serve on a jury, and humbled that I was with 11 of my peers who were intelligent, thoughtful, caring people. Court officials consisted of an alert, attentive, highly qualified judge, who guided the system very smoothly. The attorneys and their staffs showed that they were very professional, courteous and respectful of all.

The bailiff was equally efficient.

Both parties who were represented in the case were honest discerning citizens and each completely believed that their complaints were just.

Both sides made their points, making it equally hard on all involved to make a judgment.

The bottom line is that if the rest of our country's court system is as just as ours in Nacogdoches County, our country will remain the greatest in the world.

And, to paraphrase a line by one famous person[1], "We have nothing to fear, but fear itself."

---

[1] Franklin D. Roosevelt, in his Inaugural address

75. WRITER A FAN OF CLETUS HARVEY'S LETTERS TO EDITOR

I always look forward to reading Cletus Harvey's letters to the editor because they're all so positive and well-written. I only know him well enough to speak when passing him downtown, so I doubt he'd be interested in being my proofreader.

Calvin Bowden
Nacogdoches

Response:

Thank you Mr. Bowden for these words. Coming from a well known local author, they make me feel that I have accomplished something.

Cletus Harvey

76. THE DEFINITION OF INTEGRITY

An oil-boom town built upon the land owned by a huge Texas cattle ranch provided a kid with a unique education of its own.

It consisted of the necessary things: a hospital (or sorts), a drug store, grocery, a newsstand, a post office, movies (westerns), six or eight beer joints, high school, the Oracle school, and a pool hall.

The last was the most important place for a high school boy.

Some ran from school to the pool hall to get first at the table – the place filled with roughnecks, drillers, pipeliners, cowboys, and rich oil barons.

There were pool tables in the front and dominoes and moon tables in the back, with no partitions of separation.

"Mr. Big Shot", as he was known (but not to his face), would "rare" back in his chair, roll up a $100 bill, light it with a match, and then light his cigar with it.

Times were great for the healthy people who could work, but companies had no insurance coverage then, nor retirement or other benefits. If you were injured, it was up to your friends and family to care for you.

I will use the name "Claude" in the following true story.

Claude's father had been injured in an oil-field accident and had to perform odd jobs to provide for a family of five. Claude's clothes were clean, but tattered. He wore cardboard in his shoes because the soles were worn.

Pool was 10 cents a game, and we would spot him occasionally. One time "Mr. Big Shot" lit his cigar with a $100 bill, then pulled another from his pocket and yelled "Come here kid."

Claude said, "Yes, sir", put his pool stick down, and went to him.

"Here kid, take this money and go buy yourself some shoes", he said. Claude pulled himself up to his full height (probably 5 feet, 1 or 2 inches) and said quite clearly, so all could hear "My daddy will buy me some shoes, when he gets the money."

That's integrity.

Claude stayed in that town, reared a family, became a leader in the town and passed his integrity down to his people.

77. BRING IN THE RANGERS

The person who wrote the editorial Saturday, Aug. 14, defending Mr. Neza certainly has my admiration and respect.

I was one of many in Nacogdoches who were pleased that we had Joe's Italian Restaurant here. The food was excellent, the service good, and it provided employment to a number of locals, plus taxes for the city.

Again, I say that I want this to be the America I was raised in, where we stood behind and defended anyone who was trying to be a good productive citizen. Plus, this is Texas, and I was taught that the answer to any big problem was to bring in the great Texas Rangers.

So, I ask the attorney and the family of Mr. Neza to bring in our Texas Rangers.

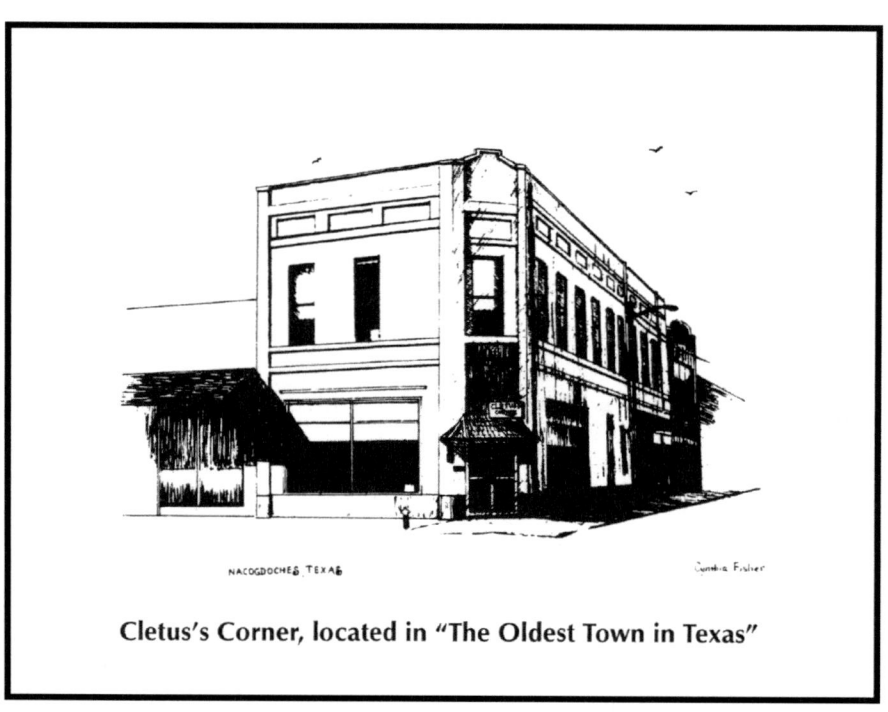

Cletus's Corner, located in "The Oldest Town in Texas"

78. DOWNTOWN MEMORIES

In about 1986, I opened a business in downtown Nacogdoches. It was in the building on the corner of Main and Pecan streets. It has almost wrap-around windows and provided the best view of all the activities in our downtown. I would arrive early so as to watch my fellow merchants open their businesses. Mr. and Mrs. Shaw would usually come around their corner first, then the Milfords at their barbershop. David and Jean Stephens at their jewelry store, Mrs. Lee Cage at the library, Richard Johnson at his café, and the lights would come on both sides of the street down East Main Street.

Johnson Furniture store was behind me. About 10 a.m., Randy's grandfather, who was in charge then, would come by the side street and wave at me on the way to do his banking business at both Stone Fort and Commercial banks. David Stephens would come out to sweep his corner and lean on his broom while he and Richard Johnson discussed all the worldly affairs.

After Randy's grandfather left us, Mr. Haden Johnson took up the torch and ran with it, and very recently Mr. Haden left us. Now his fine young son, Randy, will pick up the torch.

David Stephens left us, and now his capable son is assisting Mrs. Jean in the jewelry store.

We have always heard that ghosts have walked the streets of Nacogdoches. I will not say that I have seen some of these, but I will not say that I have not.

Some beautiful spring morning, I would like to go down to that old abandoned building, take a good position with a view, and my mind will see people, activities, and events that no one knows about but me.

79. TAKING UP FOR "REAL NACOGDOCHES TREASURES"

There has been a recent attack in the news on two of the real Nacogdoches treasures, Mr. Norman Johnson and Dr. Robert Gruebel.

Mr. Johnson spoke on his views on guns and gun control. He does not want us going through our daily lives not knowing whether some nut who had been served a bad hamburger will suddenly jerk out a gun and start shooting. Now, as to our supply of nuts, just stop at a red light, look in your rearview mirror, and watch the eyes of the person behind you sitting on your rear bumper, eyes rolling around in their head looking in their laps, faxing, texting or whatever. Then the light changes, they tear the rear end out of your automobile and, because you didn't move fast enough, pull a gun from their purse or from under the seat and start shooting because they have a permit.

Any normal person can spot a real nut case at any age. They should be reported immediately to someone around them who is considered a person of authority.

Mr. Johnson has spent a lifetime moving among people of all classes and races, entertainers, communicators, rich, poor, all religions and non-religious. Mr. Johnson is a fine man, is a man of faith, and has overcome more hard knocks than most could imagine.

Now for Dr. Robert Gruebel, a man I have personally watched try to improve the looks of our beautiful Nacogdoches for at least 25 years. I tried to make a business go in our downtown for three years. It was doomed from the start, but I didn't want to give up. I would watch Dr. Gruebel use every hour he could find (he was and is one of the most respected college professors). He would put his work clothes on and would move bricks, saw wood, hang from scaffolding – all to help improve the looks of our old town.

For at least 30 years, I have driven our visitors through town. They would see the old house on Mound Street and say "What is that?".

The answer would be that it was an old funeral home. It was near past the point of saving and needed to be bull-dozed.

Why didn't some of your people who want to leave everything as it was put your money, time, work and heart into its survival?

Writers should know the people you are bad-mouthing. Especially any of my friends (and I have a lot of good people out there).

I do not discuss topics on the phones; I do not enter into public debates. But if you could find a friend of mine who knows how to reach me, tell him to talk to me and arrange a discussion of ideas.

But you, fellow writer, should know that it is not just my friends I will try to protect. (I cannot abide any rude behavior toward any living thing).

80. MEMORY LOSS FROM RODEO FALL

Amnesia, concussion, temporary loss of memory – these things are headaches for lawyers and courts because they are so hard to prove. I personally will go on record that they can happen.

Once, years ago (I will not reveal how long) when I was a junior in high school in the little oil-patch town of Electra, Texas, I had entered the bareback riding in the Seymour, Texas, rodeo. I had a two-door black Ford I was proud of.

I loaded three couples in, and away we went. Having bought a new bareback rigging, I fully intended to return a winner.

The crowd was loud and the stands were full. Cowboys put my rigging on and I eased down on my horse. I remember about three jumps and that's it. It was lights out. I was told later that my rigging snapped. I went up a few feet and then landed on my back and the back of my head. I drove and attended the rodeo dance, distributed my passengers back home safely and went back to my home, covering some 120 miles in all.

I came to myself the next morning bent over a water fountain. I had already attended two classes and didn't remember them (that in itself was not unusual) and the last of my memory was opening that gate.

Through these years some have said that some other problem might have caused this. I always respond "just think what I might have accomplished, if it had not happened".

It has been a great life, and I would not change a thing.

81. HATES A SOGGY NEWSPAPER

Have you ever awoken to greet a Sunday morning and found a soggy paper? City beautification is wonderful. Helping the poor and needy is commendable and necessary. Preparing to bring tourism to our town is great.

But one of the most important luxuries of life is to be greeted on Sunday morning with a dry, clean, readable newspaper.

I may consult an attorney:

1. I may sue the delivery person.
2. I may sue the editor. (I hate to because he is such a fine young man.)
3. I may sue the city mayor (I don't know why, just thought that he might know something about this conspiracy.)

I have the right as an American citizen, a native Texas and taxpaying resident of the oldest town in Texas, to start a day without a soggy paper.

Editor's note: We agree. Keep the lawyers at bay and we'll fix the problem. Call circulation between 7 a.m. and 10 a.m. and we'll bring you another paper if it happens again.

82. SGT. HARVEY AND HIS LITTLE CHATTERBOX

My son Brad was special even when he was little. He would not lie if he did something wrong; he would confess. The teachers said that he had a high IQ, and he has used it in life. Through the years he faced many challenges, but fought and overcame them. Finally, he has a very happy and rewarding life. He has been a perfect son and I love him very much.

Brad & Belinda Harvey with Neil & Lacey Robinson, 1999

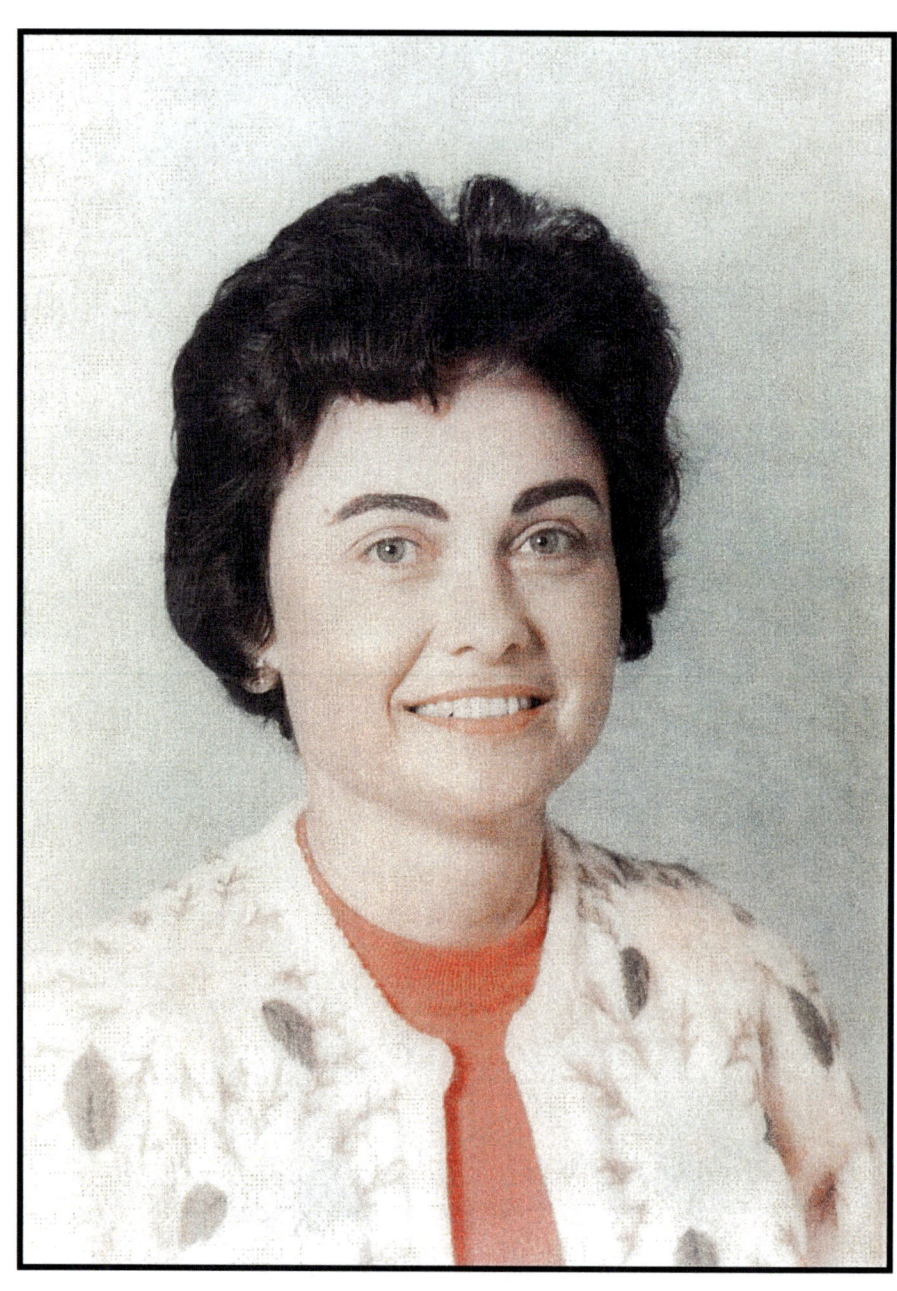

Doris Gray Harvey

83. HELPING THE LESS FORTUNATE

In the early 1970's I had bombed out and burned out in Houston, Texas.

I spotted a beautiful lady going up U.S. Hwy. 59 and I followed her to a little town.

She said I could stay if I got a job. Checking the papers I found an ad for a debit insurance salesman. I was there on a Monday. I owned two double-knit suits and looked pretty sharp.

I was hired and the first two weeks a manager showed me the territory. We went down back roads, sloughs and pig trails in conditions that most could not imagine. After that the territory became mine. The object was to collect weekly on monthly insurance and try to sell other policies. There were, and still are, some wonderful people out in the backwoods who needed and still need help. They respected themselves, their families and their neighbors, but had little means of support.

I failed as an insurance salesman.

I started going into the backwoods with the thought of helping these people. I carried them to doctors, I brought them supplies, doctored them when I could and I became important to them. I became known as the "Silver Fox". It felt great.

The company was not happy. I was slow with collections and I was not selling anything.

So, just before being fired, I quit. One lady on my route had not been to town in six months – the town being San Augustine. I thought she might be held captive but she said no, she had everything she needed and wanted and she was content.

There were two brothers who lived deep in the woods and made a little moonshine. One would walk me in to collect insurance then take me back out to the main road. Lots of stories, but only a few left to know about them.

Bill Dicks, Mike Center, Ken Gray and Danny Rowlett are a few. I would very much like to hear from them and share stories. And if the government really wants to start a helpful program, send qualified people out into the backwoods to assist people who really want to live the American dream.

Cletus Sylvester Harvey and Orville Dean Harvey

ABOUT THE AUTHOR

I was born in Pampa, Texas. I had a wonderful Mother and Father who actually liked me. My Father worked for an oil company and we soon transferred to the oil field town of Electra, Texas. Living facilities were bad in Boom Towns but because my Father worked for a major company we found housing. As a teenager, I had fun in the pool hall until the city officials decided to get me out of town by drafting me into the army. After my service ended, my life took me to the towns of Electra, Iowa Park, San Antonio, and Houston. Then I ended up in the beautiful town of Nacogdoches. This is where I want to be when the Lord calls. But it will be awhile because I have a lot of good friends up there who are telling the Lord "Don't bring him up here yet to cause trouble".

Made in the USA
San Bernardino, CA
18 December 2015